D0392507

A Christmas Cornucopia

A Christmas Cornucopia

The hidden stories behind our Yuletide traditions

Mark Forsyth

VIKING
an imprint of
PENGUIN BOOKS

VIKING

UK | USA | Canada | Ireland | Australia
India | New Zealand | South Africa

Viking is part of the Penguin Random House group
of companies whose addresses can be found at
global.penguinrandomhouse.com.

First published 2016
003

Grateful acknowledgement is made to Hodder & Stoughton
for permission to reprint an extract from 'Christmas'
by John Betjeman

Set in 10.5/15.5 pt Malabar eText
Typeset by Jouve (UK), Milton Keynes
Printed in Great Britain by Clays Ltd, St Ives plc

A CIP catalogue record for this book is available
from the British Library

ISBN: 978–0–241–26773–8

www.greenpenguin.co.uk

Contents

Preface

Picture a man sitting beside a dead tree. He is indoors and wearing a crown. From the ceiling hangs a parasitical shrub that legitimates sexual assault. He is singing to himself about a tenth-century Mittel-European murder victim using a sixteenth-century Finnish melody. Earlier, he told his children that the house had been broken into during the night by an obese Turkish man. This was a lie, but he wanted to make his children happy. Far away, in the high Andes two Peruvians are punching each other very hard indeed.

And nobody thinks that any of this is odd. Well, actually the Peruvian pugilists are a bit strange, but I'll come to them in a minute. The point is that Christmas is objectively clearly and plainly doolally. It is barmy, barking and bats. If one were to try to explain to an outsider – let's say a reasonably bright alien – what was going on, they would probably be baffled, and then blow the planet up, just to be on the safe side.

There's a lovely story about a Tokyo department store, back in the days when Christmas was unknown in Japan. The head of this store had heard rumours of a Western tradition that involved a massive shopping spree and he wanted to introduce it to Tokyo. So he sent some of his staff to investigate, and the result was that on Christmas Eve the shop's main window was decorated with a huge Santa Claus nailed to a cross.

Like all the best stories, that story is utterly untrue. But it persists, it persists because it makes us laugh, and it makes us laugh because we wonder how anything that ridiculous could happen at Christmas. When we have stopped laughing, we attach a fairy to the top of the Christmas tree and hang up our stockings by the fire.

Why? Why do we do all these strange things? Why, for a few weeks every year, do we take off our sanity, hang it neatly on the peg and dive into a sea of insanity whilst singing about how we saw three ships? Not only is it strange, what is stranger still is that we do not think it's strange. Nobody asks where these traditions come from.

Well, actually, sometimes people do ask. And they tend to come up with two answers, which utterly contradict each other.

Answer number one is that Christmas is all pagan. The lot of it. All pre-Christian stuff from thousands of years ago. The methodology for this is usually something along the lines of: 'Santa Claus has a beard. Odin had a beard. Therefore Santa Claus is Odin.' By this reasoning, Gilgamesh, the King of Ancient Uruk, is in fact Captain Birdseye, because they both have a beard and a boat.

This answer appeals for two reasons. First, it's rather romantic to think that we are carrying on a tradition that dates back thousands upon thousands of years into the dark abyss of time. Second, it makes you sound terribly well read and clever.

Answer number two is that Christmas is all Victorian. The whole festival was invented wholesale by Charles Dickens and Coca-Cola, who then used it to sell soft drinks and long novels. This answer appeals because it makes you sound terribly cynical and clever.

A good example of both of these – All Pagan! and All Victorian! – is kissing under the mistletoe. First the pagan explanation. Several very respectable books will tell you that this all goes back to the death of Baldr. Baldr was a Norse god who was killed by an arrow made of mistletoe. His mother, the unfortunately named goddess Frig, cried and her tears became the white

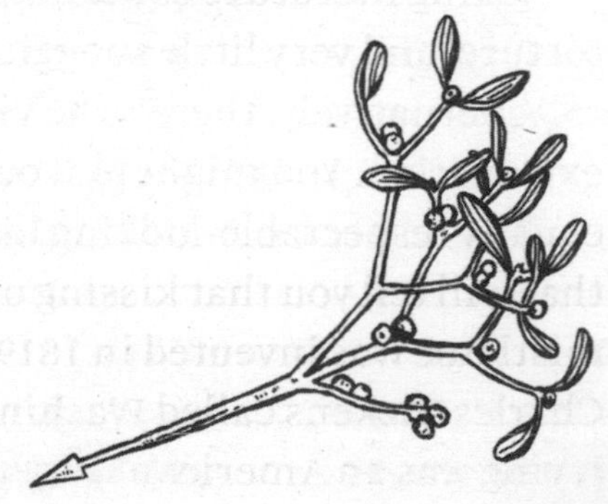

mistletoe berries. Then as her son's cadaver was being loaded onto a very flammable longship, she swore that nobody should ever again suffer from this little plant, and that we should instead kiss under it.

It's a lovely story, but if you dig out the Norse accounts of Baldr's death (there are four of them) you'll find that it's just not true. Well, the first bit is. Baldr was killed by a mistletoe arrow. That's it. The rest simply isn't there. No tears become berries. And there's certainly nothing in there about kissing. Instead, Frig is much more Norse about the whole thing. She finds the guy who made the arrow and tortures him for all eternity.

Viking literature contains an awful lot of torture, and very little snogging.

Alternatively, there's the Victorian explanation. You might pull out some equally respectable-looking history books that will tell you that kissing under the mistletoe was invented in 1819 by a friend of Charles Dickens called Washington Irving. Irving was an American writer who wrote a book (for an American audience) called *Old Christmas* about all the wonderful old yuletide traditions he had observed while staying at an English country house. In it he talks about the custom of kissing under the mistletoe.

Old Christmas was a massive bestseller, first in America and later in Britain itself. It became the standard work on How Christmas Used To Be, and therefore on How Christmas Should Be. People on both sides of the ocean read it as an instruction manual for the real, authentic, unpolluted, traditional Christmas, and then imitated it in their own homes.

However, there were some suspicious cynics who thought that Washington Irving had made most of it up. There are always cynical people in the world, and their case was substantially bolstered when Washington Irving later confessed that he had made most of it up.

But not the mistletoe. A musical came out in 1784 called *Two for One*, and one of the songs went:

When at Christmas in the hall
The men and maids are hopping,
If by chance I hear them bawl,
Amongst them quick I pop in.
What all the men, Jem, John, and Joe,
Cry, 'What good-luck has sent ye?'
And kiss beneath the mistletoe,
The girl not turned of twenty.

Washington Irving didn't make up mistletoe. Somebody must have at some point. There was a rather curious chap called Sir John Colbatch who wrote a whole book on mistletoe in 1719. But that wasn't enough. Next year, he wrote another one. His books are mainly about how he reckoned that mistletoe could cure epilepsy. But he also wrote down every other thing that he knew about mistletoe, including all the customs and superstitions associated with it. And he doesn't mention kissing. Not once.

So kissing beneath the mistletoe isn't pagan, and it isn't a Victorian invention either. It started sometime between 1720 and 1784 and I don't know why, and I never will for certain; although I can take a pretty shrewd guess that it involved a particularly lusty and inventive boy, and a particularly gullible girl.*

Of course, *some* Christmas traditions are Victorian, and *some* pagan. Let us go to Peru. Let us go to the village of Santo Tomás, twelve thousand feet above sea level, and let us imagine that it is 25 December. After a brief visit to the church, all the villagers dress up and punch each other. Really very hard. This isn't a play-fight or a ceremonial dance. This is a punch-up. Two by two, the villagers square off. Men fight men. Women fight women. There's no biting, but that's it for rules. The crowd is not allowed to get involved and, if they do, there's a man with a whip who'll whip them. This is the festival of Takanakuy.

* – Kiss me, my darling!
– No.
– But . . . but you have to.
– Why?
– Um . . . um . . . well, darling, do you see that parasitical shrub up in that tree?

The idea, apparently (and I've never hit a Peruvian, so I wouldn't know), is that it's a way of Getting It All Out Of Your System. If your neighbour has been peeving you all year, or saying unfair things about your llama, you may enter the ring, call out your neighbour's name, and attempt to pummel the living daylights out of him or her. This is, apparently, immensely therapeutic. But I imagine it's more therapeutic for the big people than the little ones. Also, you have to wear fancy dress.

Takanakuy is a good example of a festival that just happened to be on 25 December, and when Christianity and Christmas came along with its do-goody sentimental message of Love Thy Neighbour the people of Santo Tomás thought that the two would work well together.

It is vitally important when writing about traditions to remember that there are only 365 days in the year, and only so many common species of plants. Overlap is not significance. Each year, on the occasion of the Unity of Peoples of Russia and Belarus Day, I get drunk. I do this even though I am neither Russian nor Belarussian, nor particularly unified. April the 2nd just happens to be my birthday. In fact, I was born during the Grand National, but I am not a horse.

Now, I'm aware, dear reader, that I may have been a little boring in the last few paragraphs. All I have told you is that I don't know why people kiss under the mistletoe. The rest will be better. The rest will provide explanations. But I thought I should tell you the sort of nonsense that I'm not telling you. On pretty much every aspect of Christmas there are silly theories that don't have any evidence to back them up. From here on in, I'm going to tell you only what I believe to be true. At pretty much every stage I could run off blathering on about Frig and Baldr only to finish up by telling you why it's wrong. And you would quite reasonably say to yourself, 'Why am I being told of theories that aren't true? Why does he feel the need to dispel myths of which I have never heard?'

So I shan't.

One last thing, before we begin. It may seem in what follows that I am being a bit cynical, a bit mocking, that I am indulging in bah-humbuggery. Nothing could be more distant from the truth. It is true that many of our traditions are a little silly. Some of them are merely accidents. Some are, indeed, marketing ploys. Really, it doesn't matter what your traditions are. What's important is that they're there. Christmas is a great and grand Truth. It's an eternal truth even if it's a truth made of turkey and tinsel. But the great truths, the eternal ones, can only truly be grasped by mystics, by people who can see into the perfect mind of God. And these truths never shift with the seasons. They have no place and no time. But they can be grasped by the mystic in everlasting meditation. I imagine that it must be wonderful to be a mystic, if a little tiring.

For the rest of us, we need truth to have a date and a place. That way we can see it, like spray-painting the Invisible Man. We dress love up as a wedding, and death as a funeral, so that we can see them both. What is true at Christmas is true on Midsummer's Day. But we cannot see it then. Truth, for us, must have its when. Truth must have its what. We even need a how, we who are neither mystics nor angels.

And what follows has nothing to do with that truth. What follows is a why for the what, a why for the how, and a why for the when. Why do we have Christmas trees? Why do we celebrate with vast amounts of meat? And why on earth do we do it on 25 December?

1. *Why 25 December?*

Once upon a time, there was no such thing as Christmas. And then Jesus was born in Bethlehem, and after that there was still no such thing as Christmas. For hundreds of years.

The early Christian calendar was a remarkably minimalist affair. There was Easter, when you contemplated the death of the Lord, and after that there were fifty days of joyful celebration, though joyful celebration just meant praying a lot. This meant that early Christians didn't have much to do except get thrown to the lions.

Easter moves around a bit because it's meant to be held at the same time as Passover (when Jesus had His last run-in with carpentry), and Passover starts soon after the spring equinox (with a lot of complicated stuff thrown in about full moons and leap months). Being thrown to the lions, though, could happen at any time of year. And did.

When somebody got thrown to the lions (or stoned to death or crucified etc. etc.), the other Christians would note down the date of his or her death and commemorate it each year. They called it the *dies natalis*, which meant birthday, because though a martyr had died that day, he had been born in Heaven. Slowly this produced a rather doleful church calendar.

But there was no Christmas.

An important reason for this is that none of the four Gospels say what day Jesus was born. Mark and John don't mention Jesus's birth at all. Matthew and Luke do but only Luke offers any sort of clue as to the date. Luke says that shepherds were watching their flocks at night. Now shepherds only did that from March through to November. But that's a little vague.

There were other gospels around, though. The four we have in the Bible now are the four earliest surviving gospels. But there were loads of others floating about in the second century. For example, the Proto-Gospel of James (middle second century) has Mary going into labour on the way to Bethlehem and so she gives birth in a cave. Joseph hangs around outside and, at the moment that Jesus is born, he notices something rather funny:

> *. . . and I looked up into the sky, and saw the sky astonished; and I looked up to the pole of the heavens, and saw it standing, and the birds of the air keeping still. And I looked down upon the earth, and saw a trough lying, and work-people reclining: and their hands were in the trough. And those that were eating did not eat, and those that were rising did not carry it up, and those that were conveying anything to their mouths did not convey it; but the faces of all were looking upwards. And I saw the sheep walking, and the sheep stood still; and the shepherd raised his hand to strike them, and his hand remained up.*

In other words, the world is paused. That would mean that Jesus was born outside time. That would logically mean that there was No Christmas.

The apocryphal gospels are great fun and they were very popular for over a thousand years, right up until the Reformation. Then the Protestants pointed out what a lot of rubbish they were, and the Catholics decided that they didn't want to give the Protestants such an easy target and suppressed them. There's a reason they're called the apocryphal gospels: every church now ignores them. It's a shame because they have lots of great stories about Jesus's childhood, zapping school bullies and bringing dolls to life.

You can still find medieval paintings of the nativity occurring in the cave. And you can still find Christmas cards showing an ox and an ass standing over the manger or Mary riding on a donkey. There's nothing at all in the New Testament about an ox and an ass, it's from the Gospel of Pseudo-Matthew (seventh century-ish). There's also nothing at all in the Bible about Mary riding a donkey. That's from the Proto-Gospel of James.

Just to recap: there's nothing in the New Testament about what day Jesus was born. There was even an idea that his birth was so mysterious that it must be outside time. The early Christians didn't celebrate birthdays, they celebrated death days. There was even an idea that birthdays were pagan and that only pagan gods would have something so mundane as a birthday. The only birthday mentioned in the Bible is Pharaoh's, and he celebrates by hanging a baker.

Enter the Computist

So it's actually a little surprising that, from about AD 200 onwards, people did start to wonder about Jesus's birthday. Why is a mystery. They didn't have any evidence to work from, except for that detail from Luke, which none of them seems to have noticed. But they were wise enough to know that evidence is much less important than enthusiasm. And they did have three leads:

1. It was widely believed in the ancient world that great men died on their birthdays. That's because great men are neat and like to do things in round numbers.
2. It was widely believed that great events happen on anniversaries. That's because God (or the gods) is neat and likes to do things in round numbers.
3. They were prepared to do things to mathematics that it is illegal to do to animals.

With all this in mind, allow me to introduce you to the Computist. Nobody knows who the Computist was. People used to think he was St Cyprian, but then they changed their minds and started calling him Pseudo-Cyprian, which is a bit of a mouthful, so he's called the Computist for short because in AD 245 he wrote a book, and that book is all that's left of him. For all

I know, he could be a she. The book was called *On the Computation of Easter.*

It's rather hard to work out when Easter is, because it changes every year. The Bible says that Jesus was crucified on Passover Friday, and Christians were very keen on celebrating this. But the Christians could never work out when Passover was and had to keep asking the Jews, which was embarrassing. So the Computist sat down to work out all the Passovers there had ever been. He didn't have much to go on, but fortunately he was completely mad, which is always a help with difficult questions.

The Computist started with Genesis chapter 1, verse 4:

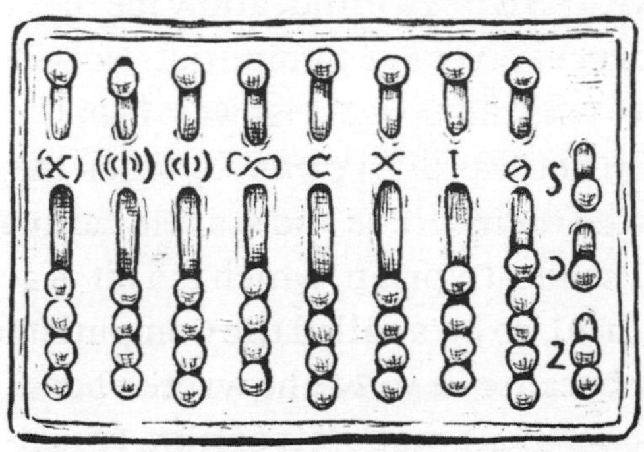

And God divided the light from the darkness.

The Computist reckoned that people who are good and fair divide things up equally. And God, who was good and fair, must therefore have made an equal amount of light and darkness. From that you can work out that the world was created on the spring equinox. He never actually explained why it was spring not autumn – presumably so the flowers would look pretty – but the point for us is that in the old calendar the spring equinox was 25 March.*

The Computist then decided that everything happened in nice round numbers. For example, great men always die on their birthday, of course. He then

* There's an awful lot of complicated stuff that I should explain about the difference between the Julian and Gregorian calendars and the precession of the equinoxes, but I haven't the heart, and you would be bored to weeping. Just take it from me that that's when the spring equinox was. If you want to learn more about the various dating systems, I pity you.

worked out every Passover from Exodus onwards and found that his numbers didn't add up. But luckily for the Computist, he was mad.

So he started adding in numbers here and taking them away there and making interesting statements like 'seven weeks comprise forty-nine years'. And then he added up the letters in Jesus's name and decided he was allowed to subtract them (or sometimes add them). And thus he worked out that Jesus was crucified on 9 April, and that He had been born on 28 March.

But it occurs to me, dear reader, that you may think that I'm making this all up as I go along. So let me quote you a little passage. If you can read the following without needing a stiff drink and a lie down, you're a better human being than I am.

> *Accordingly, as a secret symbol of Christ, a hundred were first deducted from the 434 years, and there remained 334. The 300 years, it is clear, showed T, the sign of the Cross. There remained thirty-four.*

From them three were deducted because of the day of the Resurrection, and there remained thirty-one. On their completion it behoved Christ to suffer for the sins of the believers. Let us then add these 434 years to the sum obtained above, and we find from the Exodus to the birth of Christ 1548 years. Desiring to learn the time of this birth, let us carefully count these 1548 years from the Exodus, i.e. from the first line of the pinax, and we shall arrive at the day of His nativity. That day being in the sixth sedecennitas in the thirteenth line is found to be 28 March, a Wednesday!

O the splendid and divine providence of the Lord, that on that day, even the very day, on which the sun was made, 28 March, a Wednesday, Christ should be born! For this reason Malachi the prophet, speaking about him to the people, fittingly said:

Unto you shall the sun of righteousness arise, and healing is in his wings.

Is that crystal clear? Splendid.

Now you might think that the Computist had solved the problem once and for all. But various other people got on to the question. They all reasoned in roughly the same way (really). And all placed Jesus's birth in the spring, all working it out from the equinox. Some said 2 April, some 19 April; 25 March pops up for reasons that look almost sane.

What's important here is that Christmas is always on or soon after 25 March. So, if Christ came into the world on 25 March, why was He born nine months later?

That question should pretty much have answered itself; if it hasn't, consult a grown-up. Or indeed, check on a church calendar under 25 March and you will find the Feast of the Annunciation, when Mary was told that she was up the spout.

'Wait a damned minute,' I hear you cry. 'The Computist said that the *nativity* was 25 March. Not the conception.' And you're right but the Computist was *theologically wrong*. In fact, he may even have been a heretic.

Just as the early Christians were a little confused about what was a proper gospel and what wasn't, they were also rather lackadaisical on how Jesus became Christ. One very popular view was that Jesus was the *adopted* son of God. The idea is that Jesus was an ordinary, if rather virtuous, human being until the day that He was baptized, aged about thirty. Then the voice of God in the heavens said, 'Thou art my son,' meaning, 'As of now, thou art my son.'

Adoptionism's actually a rather neat theory, because it gets rid of all those questions about what Jesus was doing before He started curing lepers and feeding thousands. What was His childhood like? Was He ever a naughty boy? Did He cure all the other children at school? If not, why not?

All solved if you say that Jesus became Christ at His baptism.

The second theory is that Jesus was Christ from the moment of His birth. On the face of it, this is a nice, plain straight-up-and-down way of looking at things. But it leaves you with the question of what was in

Mary's womb from the point that the Holy Ghost did whatever it did up until the birth. It also rather does down the Virgin Mary. She gets to suckle the Messiah, but she never got to gestate Him.

And if there's one thing Christians of the second century were sure of, it's that they were becoming increasingly keen on the Virgin Mary. If she didn't have Christ in her womb, then she's something of a bit-part. She pretty much drops out of the story as soon as she appears. But if she spent nine months with God growing inside her, then she contained the mystery of the incarnation.

Anyway, the question was soon solved, because in 313 the Emperor Constantine the Great announced that the Christians should no longer be persecuted by pagans, and that they could now get on with persecuting each other. And in 325 he called a great council at Nicaea so that they could decide exactly what they were going to persecute each other about. They decided that Adoptionism was wrong.

And so it was decided that Jesus was *conceived* on 25 March and Christmas was moved forward precisely nine months from the spring equinox to the winter solstice. The first record of this date is in a book called *Chronography* of AD 354, and that's what it's been ever since.* The date had probably been around for a few decades before that. It's just that the *Chronography* is the first book to survive.

You can even work out the precise time of day He was born, if you scour the Old Testament thoroughly enough. All you need to do is read The Book of Wisdom, chapter 18, verse 14:

> *While gentle silence enveloped all things, and night in its swift course was now half gone, thy all-powerful word leaped from heaven, from the royal throne, into the midst of the land that was doomed.*

* The Eastern Orthodox churches still use the Julian calendar (see previous footnote), which means that 25 December is 7 January.

Midnight. Which is why we go to Midnight Mass. This is especially neat as it means Jesus was born in the middle of the night, on the longest night of the year.* The poor Computist might even have been pleased.

Saturnalia, Sol Invictus and the Kalends

The Romans loved their feasts, festivals and holidays. It's hard to count them all, but by the third century there were about two hundred of them per year. This means that, although 25 December had been worked out from rather arbitrary biblical sources, when Christmas moved in, it found that it had some noisy neighbours.

The big problem was the Feast of the Unconquered Sun, which the Romans called Sol Invictus. This was celebrated on the winter solstice. All through the year the sun got lower and lower in the sky at noon until

* As before, precession of equinoxes, Julian/ Gregorian calendar etc.

on 25 December it got to its lowest point,* stopped descending, and started going up again. That, incidentally, is where the word solstice comes from: *sol* means sun, and *sistere* means stop. Sun worship was a big thing in the Roman Empire at the time and sun worshippers had already staked out 25 December as their festival.

Then there was Saturnalia. Saturnalia was essentially a great big winter booze-up that lasted from 17 to 23 December. It was a confusing time. Slave-owners would pretend to be slaves, slaves would pretend to be slave-owners, and nobody seemed to find that weird.

Finally, there was the Kalends of January. *Kalends* just means the first day of the month and it's where we get the word *calendar* from. The Romans made a reasonably big fuss of the Kalends of January and used to give each other presents.

* Ditto. Look, if you really are interested, there's a book called *Mapping Time: The Calendar and Its History* by E. G. Richards. Good introduction to the subject and it's only 464 pages long.

Now there are some people who say that Christmas was put on 25 December just so that it could replace the festival of Sol Invictus, which happened to be on the same day. This is extraordinarily unlikely as nobody mentions the idea at all until over 800 years later, and because the festival of Sol Invictus is first recorded in . . . wait for it . . . the *Chronography* of AD 354, the same book that first mentioned Christmas on 25 December. Some people say that Christmas is really Saturnalia, which is even less likely because they're on different dates. What is true is that the new festival of Christmas had competition.

But the Christians knew that they had competition, so they tried their very best to point out that they were different. St Augustine tried to make fun of the pagans by saying that they worshipped the sun on 25 December, but Christians worshipped He who created the sun. St Ambrose tried a similar line, saying that 'Christ is *our* new sun.'

The important thing is that all these

saints and bishops were really trying to push Christmas. They were trying to sell this utterly new festival that nobody had heard of a few decades before. They had to do that because they had to knock out the pagan competition, and because December Christmas was a way to stamp out Adoptionism.

And they were successful. They were so successful that by AD 386 Christmas was already being described as 'the mother of all festivals'. And a chap called Gregory of Nazianzus was already starting with that old familiar complaint that Christmas was filled with 'feasting to excess, dancing and crowning the doors' and that we should all get back to the proper spiritual meaning. Bah humbug.

In fact, there are two really important things that will pop up with tedious regularity in pretty much every chapter of this book: (1) There's really nothing in the Bible to justify 25 December; (2) Christmas has always, and I mean always . . . all right, I mean from AD 386 onwards . . . Christmas has for sixteen hundred years been viewed as a festival that has lost sight of its True Meaning.

Oh, and there's another thing: that Council of Nicaea when they decided that Adoptionism was wrong, thus spurring the celebration of Christmas? One of the delegates at the council was almost certainly a fellow called Nicholas of Myra, who had no idea that it would start a chain of events that resulted in him flying around the earth on a sleigh drawn by reindeer and leaving presents beside an indoor tree.

2. *The Christmas Tree*

A proper Christmas tree should have a snake in it, and if it doesn't have a snake in it, it's not a proper Christmas tree. You may think that I'm being a little odd, dear reader, but you're the one with a dead tree in your house, and you don't even know why.

Christmas trees are one of those classic cases where people will either say 'It must be Victorian' or 'It must be pagan'. Both views are utterly, utterly wrong. The pre-Christian pagans of northern Europe did worship trees, but they worshipped oak trees, and they worshipped them all year round, and they worshipped them outdoors. There are a lot of trees in the world – what makes the Christmas tree different is that it's indoors in midwinter and it's decorated with baubles. However, the explanation for all this is actually surprisingly simple, it's just that we have to go back (as so often in this book) to the creation of the world.

Notwithstanding the spoilsport theories of Charles Darwin, our great-great-great (roughly 240 greats) grandparents were Adam and Eve. They did something naughty involving fruit, probably because they were naked, and then they were chucked out of the Garden of Eden. And then what?

Well, aside from a couple of begettings, they pretty much disappear from the Bible. What happened to them afterwards? Now, you may think that nobody knows and nobody can know because there's nothing in the Bible. But details like that never bothered the medieval faithful because in medieval times there was a biography of Adam and Eve and what they did next. Of course it's completely made up, but it's great fun, especially if you're a raging misogynist.

Basically, Eve goes and does it again. She's like Laurel to Adam's Hardy. Once they're out of the Garden of Eden, Adam realizes that they'll be able to get back into Paradise if they only do a penance, and he has a perfect penance in mind. They'll both go and stand in a river for forty days and forty nights and at the end of that God will forgive them. So he goes and stands in the Euphrates and Eve goes and stands in the Tigris (sometimes it's the other way around, there were lots of different versions of the story), and they both wait. This worries the Hell out of the Devil, or rather it worries the Devil out of Hell, and so after thirty-nine days he disguises himself as an angel and pays a visit to his old chum Eve. She's up to her neck in the river when he arrives and he tells her that he's been sent from God to tell her that her penance is done. Eve jumps out of the river, towels herself off, and goes to tell Adam the good news. Adam sees what's happened and that's that for humanity: Original Sin was there to stay.

There's also some other stuff about who was the midwife for Cain and Abel (an angel) and how did Adam get the seeds to start farming (angel) and where did Eve get the spinning wheel to make clothes for herself and her family (angel). It basically answers all the common sense questions medieval people would have about how on earth Adam and Eve survived on earth. And the answer is always an angel.

Adam and Eve were a much bigger deal to medieval people than they are to us. They were even venerated as saints. They weren't official saints, but they did have a name-day. And guess which day that was?

Before I tell you, I should mention another reason that Adam and Eve were important to the medievals. Medieval people loved the Virgin Mary. This is hardly surprising, a lot of people still do. But the problem with loving the Virgin Mary is that, like Adam and Eve, she's got a massive part in the nativity story, and then she pretty much disappears, aside from the occasional pop-up-to-look-at-her-son moments.

This veneration of the Virgin is (as we've seen elsewhere) a big reason for celebrating Christmas. Christmas is the thing, the only thing, that makes Mary important. Because it's at Christmas that Mary undoes all the trouble by giving birth to the New Adam.

Theologically, it's terribly important that Adam (and Eve) cursed humankind and Jesus (and Mary) redeemed them. St Paul loves to go on about this:

> *For since by man came death, by man came also the resurrection of the dead. For as in Adam all die, even so in Christ shall all be made alive.* (1 Cor. 15:21–2)

So Adam fell by Eve, and Christ was born of Mary on 25 December. The one answered the other. So Adam and Eve's name day was 24 December.

The other thing that medieval Christians liked was plays. This was something to do with most of them not being able to read. But even priests, who could read, liked plays. They particularly liked plays telling stories from the Bible and other odd books like the biography of Adam and Eve. They would put them on in church, and they got so enthusiastic that in 1210 the Pope banned all priests from acting on stage because it was beginning to look undignified.

So the plays simply got a new cast. Usually it was members of guilds who would perform the biblical stories. The guilds were just groups of people who worked in the same profession and understood the mysteries of metalwork or haberdashery or whatever it happened to be. So the guilds were sometimes called 'mysteries' and the plays were called 'mystery plays'.

These existed all over Europe. There is a complete surviving set from York and another from Wakefield. But they were everywhere. Often, a complete cycle would be performed at Easter telling the whole story of the world from creation to crucifixion. Other plays would be performed on a particular saint's day. For example, the plays about St Nicholas (see chapter 5) were staged on 6 December.

And a lot of these plays were about Adam and Eve and the fall of man and the incident in the river. These ones were called Paradise Plays. What did these performances look like? Well, unfortunately medieval plays almost never have stage directions. But one does. It's called *Le Jeu d'Adam* and it was the Paradise Play of Arras in northern France. And it tells you everything.

First of all, the disappointing news. Adam and Eve were not naked. Despite the fact that the Bible absolutely insists that they were nudists until they ate the apple.

> *Adam shall wear a red tunic, but Eve a woman's garment in white with a white silk scarf; and they shall both stand in front of God – Adam, however, nearer to God with a calm countenance, Eve with face lowered.*

Then, when they've fallen, they still wear clothes, just rather shabbier ones. But what about the rest of the staging? What is the one thing you absolutely need for a play about the Garden of Eden? You need a tree. You need a tree decorated with apples. And the stage directions of *Le Jeu d'Adam* quite specifically describe it and its purpose:

> *Then shall a serpent, cunningly contrived, climb up the trunk of the*

forbidden tree; Eve shall put her ear up to it as if listening to its advice. Then Eve shall take the apple and offer it to Adam.

A tree decorated with fruit was an essential part of the Paradise Play. And Paradise Plays lasted. They were popular all over northern France and north-west Germany until the Reformation, when the fun, as usual, had to stop. But they survived in one strange place called Oberufer.

Oberufer was a little island in the Danube in the middle of Hungary. It's odd because in the sixteenth century it was colonized by Germans. Nobody's quite sure why the Germans set off into the middle of

Hungary but they did, and they settled there, and they remained there as a strange untouched relic. They didn't talk much to the outside world and the outside world didn't talk much to them. And they kept performing their Paradise Play. They were still performing their Paradise Play when they were found by a linguist and scholar called Karl Schröer in the nineteenth century.

The scripts had been handed down for generations. The play was performed on Christmas Eve, indoors, with the whole village attending, and on the stage there was a tree decorated with apples and ribbons.

But it survived only in Oberufer. In Germany itself the Paradise Plays were pretty much killed by the Reformation. But the tree survived, and in some areas it is still called the *Paradeisbaum*, even though people have forgotten why. The Christmas tree is just a stage prop.

The earliest recorded Christmas tree was in Freiburg in 1419, in the Hospital of the Holy Spirit. It was decorated with apples, wafers, gingerbreads and tinsel. After that you have scattered references, mainly to them being banned. The problem with going out and cutting down a Christmas tree was that it probably belonged to someone else. They were banned in Strasbourg in 1494 and Freiburg in 1554. In 1561 a law in Alsace limited each family to 'one pine in the length of eight shoes'. But Christmas trees were geographically limited. They appear to have been really popular only in north-west Germany and north-east France. Apart from one mysterious outlier.

The First English Christmas Tree

The very first Christmas tree in England is a complete mystery, and it was torn down by the Devil. Or at least that's the story. It pops up in John Stow's *Survey of London*, which was written in 1598, but describes how:

> *in the year 1444 by tempest of thunder and lightning on the 1st of February at night Paul's steeple was fired but with great*

labour quenched, and towards the morning of Candlemas Day at the Leaden hall in Cornhill a standard of tree being set up in midst of the pavement fast in the ground nailed full of holm and ivy for disport of Christmas to the people was torn up and cast down by the malignant spirit as was thought, and the stones of the pavement all about were cast in the streets and into divers houses so that the people were sore aghast of the great tempests.

It's all rather enigmatic. Were there Paradise Plays in London? It's possible, but none has been recorded, and there may be many other disports of Christmas that have been lost to history. If it was a proper Christmas tree it was a one-off, as they remained a German thing for centuries. When Germans went abroad they pined for home and indoor pine trees. So, the first reference to candles on the trees comes from the German wife of the Duke of Orléans in 1708. And Christmas trees properly arrived in Britain with our most famous German immigrants: the royal family. George III's wife had a Christmas tree because her name was Charlotte of Mecklenburg-Strelitz, and with a name like that you have to be German. Queen Victoria had Christmas trees as a child, and then she married a German and had more Christmas trees, and then in 1848 the *Illustrated London News* published a picture of the royal family gathered around their tree and at that moment trees got big in Britain.

A couple of years later Charles Dickens (who was in charge of English Christmases at the time) wrote a whole essay on the subject that began thus:

> *I have been looking on, this evening, at a merry company of children assembled round that pretty German toy, a Christmas Tree. The tree was planted in the middle of a great round table, and towered high above their heads. It was brilliantly lighted by a multitude of little tapers; and everywhere sparkled and glittered with bright objects. There were*

rosy-cheeked dolls, hiding behind the green leaves; and there were real watches (with movable hands, at least, and an endless capacity of being wound up) dangling from innumerable twigs; there were French-polished tables, chairs, bedsteads, wardrobes, eight-day clocks, and various other articles of domestic furniture (wonderfully made, in tin, at Wolverhampton), perched among the boughs, as if in preparation for some fairy housekeeping; there were jolly, broad-faced little men, much more agreeable in appearance than many real men – and no wonder, for their heads took off, and showed them to be full of sugar-plums; there were fiddles and drums; there were tambourines, books, work-boxes, paint-boxes, sweetmeat-boxes, peep-show boxes, and all kinds of boxes; there were trinkets for the elder girls, far brighter than any grown-up gold and jewels; there were baskets and pincushions in all devices; there were guns, swords, and banners; there were witches standing in

> *enchanted rings of pasteboard, to tell fortunes; there were teetotums, humming-tops, needle-cases, pen-wipers, smelling-bottles, conversation-cards, bouquet-holders; real fruit, made artificially dazzling with gold leaf; imitation apples, pears, and walnuts, crammed with surprises; in short, as a pretty child, before me, delightedly whispered to another pretty child, her bosom friend, 'There was everything, and more.'*

A *teetotum*, since you ask, is a spinning top with letters on its sides. And a *peep-show box* in that more innocent age was a box with a magnifying glass in the side through which you could see little painted wonders. In the twentieth century some bright and drooling spark had the idea of putting dirty pictures inside, and eventually somebody decided to shove a whole woman in there. This is called Progress.

The Christmas tree was now properly British and the most popular decoration for the very top was neither an angel nor a star, but a Union Jack. Nonetheless, to this very day, the *Oxford English Dictionary* defines a Christmas tree as:

> *A famous feature of Christmas celebration in Germany, frequently but imperfectly imitated in England.*

But all Christmas trees are imperfect imitations of the original, unless they contain a snake. So, alas, the true Christmas tree is gone, almost gone. The last recorded proper Christmas tree was in Swindon in the year 2000. It was bought by a Mrs Coulson who was halfway through putting it up when she was bitten by an adder that had been hibernating in it. The tree later turned out to contain three snakes.

This must count as a miracle, a sign from God. But nobody seemed to notice and Mrs Coulson herself announced solemnly, 'Next year I will be getting a plastic tree.'

And now that the Christmas tree is up, we know that it's Advent.

3. *Advent*

Almost everybody knows that Advent begins on the first day of December, and almost everybody is wrong. Or they're wrong six years out of seven. Advent begins on the Sunday nearest to 30 November, which is St Andrew's Day. A hundred years ago everybody would have known this, and the reason so many people get it wrong is down to one German chap called Gerhard Lang, or you can, if you like, blame his mother.

Mrs Lang used to make Advent calendars for her son Gerhard. This wasn't new. Home-made Advent calendars had been around in Germany since the 1850s, and before that people had lit candles or crossed off chalk markings. But Mrs Lang was particularly inventive with hers, apparently because her son was particularly obsessed with Christmas. Really, the Advent calendar was, and is, a way for parents to forestall the endless questions from children of 'Are we there yet?'

Mrs Lang would attach sweets to her advent calendar with string, and Gerhard would get to eat one sweet every day. Then he grew up and became a publisher, which was a double tragedy.

In 1908 Lang became the first person to mass produce Advent calendars. Previously, they had all been made by solicitous (or irritated) *Hausfrauen*. But, apart from one that appeared in a newspaper, this was the first time that they had been mass produced, and the thing about mass production is that it needs standardization. If Lang had insisted on his calendars beginning on the nearest Sunday to St Andrew's Day, he would have had to make a new design every year, and wouldn't have been able to sell last year's stock. So from the 1920s onwards he just stuck to 1 December, and so most of us do as well.

Almost everybody knows that Advent is about the coming of Christmas, and almost everybody is wrong. Or at least half wrong.

'Advent' certainly means 'coming'. It's from the Latin *adventus* (coming), and it's the same -vent you find in *circumvent* (come around), *prevent* (come before), *invent* (come to, hence discover), and *adventure* (which was originally a chance, hence whatever came up). But Advent is not primarily about the coming of Christ, it's about the Second Coming, the fun one when, according to Luke 21:25–7:

> *... there will be signs in sun and moon and stars, and on the earth distress of nations in perplexity because of the roaring of the sea and the waves, people fainting with fear and with foreboding of what is coming on the world. For the powers of the heavens will be shaken. And then they will see the Son of Man coming in a cloud with power and great glory.*

And that is the reading for Advent Sunday.* Very traditional priests will insist

* Technically, the readings change on a three-year cycle: Luke 21, Matthew 24 and Mark 13. Each one is wildly apocalyptic.

that the first two weeks are entirely about preparing yourself for the last judgement, and that you don't get to think about Christmas until the third Sunday.

Anyway, almost everybody knows that Advent is the beginning of the Christmas season, and they're wrong too. According to the church calendar, the Christmas period begins at dusk on Christmas Eve and lasts for twelve days to the feast of Epiphany when the Magi arrived. Or you can argue it lasts until 2 February. It depends on which priest you ask and how fond they are of incense. Importantly, this means that you shouldn't start singing Christmas hymns until 24 December (sunset), and you should still be singing them in early January. There are still vicars who insist upon this.

Anyway, everybody at least knows that Advent is the bit of time before Christmas. Originally, though, it wasn't. Advent was originally the other Lent, it was the forty days of fasting before the feast of Epiphany on 6 January.

But anyway, Advent, whatever it is and

however you date it, is upon us. And you are going to have to settle down and do Advent stuff like cards and shopping.

Cards

Christmas cards are, without doubt, the most annoying custom of Christmas. They can be blamed on one man: Sir Henry Cole. Cole did some good things with his life: he was instrumental in setting up the British national penny-post system with a single stamp that would take a letter to anywhere in the country. But, four years later, he ruined it all by commissioning the first Christmas card from the artist John Callcott Horsley. Actually, he only ruined it for the rich in London (which is something of a reversal of the natural order); the original Christmas card cost a shilling, which was about a day's wage for a manual labourer. Each one had to be printed in black and white and then coloured in by hand. The picture showed a jolly family sitting around a table looking out at you as though you were there, or they wanted you to be there. The genial patriarch looks very like Henry Cole. The children are all drinking wine, which is something.

Less than a thousand copies of the original were sold. But unfortunately for everybody, printing techniques were improving. Soon Christmas cards were expected from the middle classes, and eventually even the poor spat-upon proletariat. They really took off in the 1870s with the introduction of the halfpenny post, which meant everybody was now in on the chore.

You will occasionally hear people complain that Christmas cards have become too secular. Where's the lovely image of a man nailed to a cross? But the Victorian originals were secular – secular and weird. A favourite theme was animals dressed up as humans, or Christmas puddings come to life, or terrifying snowmen, or frogs. Lots of frogs. Frogs dancing, frogs murdering each other. Looking at Victorian Christmas cards is like studying the foul unconscious of a gentleman psychopath. Violent frogs, sad-eyed children, and owls in top hats. It is

little wonder that a man called Louis Prang was able to introduce them with ease to the United States.

But weirdest of all are the naked girls. This may have something to do with the fact that Valentine cards had been around for ages and card manufacturers were just trying to sell off stock. But most of them would get you arrested these days and put on some sort of register.

However, for some people the Christmas card was not hideous enough. The tiresome business of signing and sending a picture of a demented dog in a hat to everybody they knew was just not sufficiently tedious.

These people needed to write a Round Robin. This is entirely unrelated to the robins which infest our faux Victorian Christmas Cards, for which, see Chapter 6.

A round robin was originally a naval tradition, and the idea was that you could send a letter without making people hate you (how times have changed!). Imagine you're a sailor on the brink of mutiny; not too hard, is it? You wish to give a final ultimatum to your captain. But nobody wants to be the first to speak out because the first to speak out will probably be clapped in irons or keelhauled or made to walk the plank, or all three simultaneously. The captain just needs to make an example of the ringleader. Even if you don't speak out, even if you write a letter, he'll probably just do it to the *first* person to add their signature.

So, wishing to avoid the lash, you write a round robin, in which every sailor signs their name in a big circle. The captain, when he gets it, won't know who signed first and won't be able to make everybody walk the plank, so you're safe.

It is unclear exactly how this tradition of naval mutiny transferred itself to Christmas letters, but it did. In fact, it reversed itself, so instead of one letter with lots of signatures, it became lots of letters with one signature. It may have something to do with the fact that Victorian postmen were sometimes called 'Robins'. Nobody's really sure.

Anyway, that is why you receive those precious updates about little Gwendoline and her oboe lessons and her school prizes and her swimming certificate, which will come every year with the dismal regularity of a tax bill until they suddenly cease when little Gwendoline grows up and starts smoking crack.

Shopping

The sweet and silly Christmas things,
Bath salts and inexpensive scent
And hideous ties so kindly meant.

John Betjeman, 'Christmas'

You almost certainly made a loss on your Christmas shopping. By that I mean that when you add up the value of all the presents you received from your friends and relations (never the twain shall meet) and then subtract the amount that you spent, you end up in the red. So does everybody else, which is curious. You may be thinking here that this must come down to children, those small people who receive presents but, because of fashionable child-labour laws, are unable to contribute. But you make a loss anyway, even if you don't count the children. This is because of what economists call a *deadweight loss*.

The principle is pretty simple. Let's say that you really, really want a pair of stripy socks. In fact, you want them so much that you would be prepared to pay £10 for such a wonderful thing. You would not pay that much for polka-dot socks. You aren't that fond of polka-dot socks. You would never pay more than a fiver for polka-dot socks. So stripy socks are worth a tenner to you, spotty socks are worth a fiver. That is their value *to you*. But your sister-in-law does not know this.

Your sister-in-law thinks that you'd probably really like some spotty socks. So she goes out and spends a tenner on what she foolishly believes is a really nice pair. Then she gives them to you. Effectively, between the two of you, you just lost a fiver. That's what happens when you let somebody else go and do your buying for you. The problem is that you have almost certainly done the same with her present. So, between the two of you, you've lost another fiver. That's deadweight loss.

The only way to iron out this economic inefficiency would be to have perfect information. If you could only know everything about the other's tastes and what the other was planning to buy, all would be well. Luckily for us though, there is the age-old tradition that your present should be a surprise, which absolutely guarantees that everybody loses out. Clever economists who have done the maths and worked it all out reckon that there's about four billion dollars of deadweight loss in the USA every Christmas. That's enough to buy a modestly sized aircraft carrier, or 1.1 billion pairs of socks.

But you must do it nonetheless. As early as possible. On 26 November 1923 *The Times* reported that:

> *The Queen and Princess Mary, Viscountess Lascelles, have done a considerable portion of their shopping already. They began the buying of toys (of which both make large purchases each year) some weeks ago, and last week the Queen did a good deal of general buying, and thus set a good example to the rest of London.*

The reason that it was your patriotic duty to get your shopping done early is that the crowds in central London were already a major transport problem in the twenties. The new-fangled Tube allowed everyone to come down and gawp at the Christmas lights. Gone were the simpler days of simpler presents. Back in 1688 Samuel Pepys recorded that:

> *The Friends of Mr. Tierney at Colchester, have sent him as a Christmas present, a small Barrel of Oysters – that will not open.*

But if you really want to splash out, and you have the time, money and a highly trained army, you could follow the example of General Sherman in the American Civil War. He had been incommunicado for a few weeks and Lincoln was getting rather antsy, until, on 22 December, he received a telegram saying:

> *I beg to present you, as a Christmas gift, the city of Savannah, with 150 heavy guns and plenty of ammunition, and also about 25,000 bales of cotton.*

And with all that cotton, you could probably make an awful lot of socks. The only way to go one up on that is to take the route of Pope Leo III, who crowned Charlemagne Roman Emperor as a Christmas surprise. But this is hard for people of average income and little army to achieve. So if you can't rule the

Western world, I can only inform you that, whilst researching this book, I met a lady who had spent her career organizing the Christmas selections of one of the major British department stores. She told me that the big seasonal seller was chocolate body paint.

But do not smear it on yourself just yet. Advent is nearly over. It is Christmas Eve. It is time to go to church.

4. *Christmas Carols*

The Christmas carol service was invented in Truro in 1880 by a chap called Edward White Benson. The story goes that on Christmas Eve everybody in Truro would get disgustingly drunk, and that the Bishop of Truro (Benson) was so disgusted that he decided to lure everybody out of the pub and into the church with his new service.

The problem with this story is that there's no evidence that that's what motivated Benson. And we do know a lot about him. He later became Archbishop of Canterbury and his whole family had something of a mania for writing. His wife had thirty-nine lesbian lovers. How do we know that? Because she kept a diary, and numbered them. One of his sons was the eminent gay novelist E. F. Benson. Another was the eminent gay poet Arthur Benson.

Arthur wrote the words to 'Land of Hope and Glory'. He also wrote a diary of four million words, which is often reckoned to be the longest ever.* Edward's daughter Margaret was an eminent lesbian Egyptologist. His daughter Nellie actually stole one of her own mother's girlfriends and died of TB.

Astoundingly, there were no grandchildren.†

Anyway, in 1880 this family, or rather this hive of oversexed logomania, was in the brand-new diocese of Truro. It was so brand new that they didn't even have a cathedral, just a large shed, and Edward White Benson decided to invent the carol service, perhaps not to get the people out of the pubs, but to get the carols out.

You see, before this, Christmas carols

* That's more than four times the length of the complete works of Shakespeare.

† This seems to have been quite a normal family for the head of the Church of England. After Benson died his wife shacked up with a woman called Lucy Tait, who was the daughter of the previous Archbishop of Canterbury.

hadn't been sung in the church, they'd been sung in the pub. Carols were folk songs; originally they were folk dances (that's what 'carol' meant: 'a dance in a ring'). This is why so many of them are really rather odd. Why would you see three ships come sailing by? The answer is that nobody knows. It was just a song that in some versions involved Jesus on Christmas day in the morning, and in other versions involved three pretty girls on New Year's Day. It doesn't make any sense anyway as a Christmas hymn because Bethlehem is landlocked. The same thing goes for 'The Holly and the Ivy'. There is a religious version, but there are also versions that are just about holly and ivy, and the fascinating question of which one is better.

Then in the eighteenth and nineteenth centuries folklorists started to collect these folk songs and smarten them up, and people started to write new ones. But even these new ones were a bit incoherent and the versions changed all the time. For example, the co-founder of Methodism Charles Wesley wrote a beautiful carol that began:

Hark how all the welkin rings
Glory to the King of Kings
Peace on earth and mercy mild
God and sinners reconciled.

And that's how the carol went for twenty years, until another preacher called George Whitefield published a new version that went:

Hark, the herald angels sing
Glory to the new-born King!

Wesley was not in the slightest bit amused by this (probably because the Bible is quite clear that the herald angels who appear to the shepherds *say* their news, they don't sing it). He wrote:

Many gentlemen have done my brother
and me (though without naming us)
the honour to reprint many of our hymns.
Now they are perfectly welcome to do so
provided they print them just as they are.
But I desire they would not attempt to
mend them; for they really are not able.

He goes on to say that he doesn't want to be held 'accountable either for the nonsense or for the doggerel of other men'. But he is. Look in any hymnbook and 'Hark the Herald Angels Sing' will be clearly listed: words by Wesley, tune by Mendelssohn.

Mendelssohn would be even more perplexed and vexed by the whole thing. He died without ever even hearing of the hymn. All he did was to write a song about Gutenberg. It was precisely 400 years since the invention of the printing press and Mendelssohn knocked out a song about it. However, he realized that once the anniversary had passed, it would probably need some new words as songs about type aren't that popular. He wrote in a letter that he didn't mind what new words were written just so long as they weren't religious. Then he died, and a few years later somebody noticed that the tune would work very well with 'Hark the Herald Angels Sing' and that was that. And ever since then people have been carolling away unaware that they are going against the explicit, written wishes of both the lyricist and the composer.

'Good King Wenceslas' is an even odder business. Good King Wenceslas was a real chap, except he wasn't a king and he wasn't called Wenceslas, but he may have been good. His name was Vaclav and he was Duke of Bohemia in the tenth century. Poor little Vaclav had a difficult childhood. His father died when he was a child and he was brought up partly by his mother and partly by his paternal grandmother. These two ladies did not get along at all well, especially as his mother was pagan and his grandma was Christian. Eventually, his mother solved the problem by the time-honoured method of dealing with difficult mothers-in-law: she had her assassinated – strangled with a veil, to be precise. Then Vaclav came of age and employed the time-honoured method of dealing with overbearing mothers: he exiled her.

After that Vaclav started his career of do-goodery. He would potter about his

dukedom, especially at night, giving stuff to the poor. An early biography says:

> *Rising every night from his noble bed, with bare feet and only one chamberlain, he went around to God's churches and gave alms generously to widows, orphans, those in prison and afflicted by every difficulty, so much so that he was considered, not a prince, but the father of all the wretched.*

Given that he was the duke, I would have thought that he could just free the prisoners. And I don't think much of prisons that anybody can break into in the middle of the night. Mind you, I also don't see what he had against shoes; and I shall never know now that he's dead.

You see, Vaclav still had one family member left, his brother Boleslaus the Cruel. Now, if I had a brother with a name like that, I would watch out. It's a dead giveaway. I would employ bodyguards. I would watch my back like a hawk. But Vaclav didn't and Boleslaus and a few of his friends assassinated him in 935. It is a sad truth, but a certain one, that Good King Wenceslas did *not* look out.

But where (I hear you cry) was Wenceslas' faithful page in all this, the one who followed him around in the snow? Well, his name was Podevin and he doesn't seem to have been there at the assassination; instead he showed his Christian charity by taking out one of the assassins in a revenge killing before being chased, cornered in a forest, and killed.

He wasn't the only one. In 1982 a mass grave was discovered near Prague containing the bodies of sixty soldiers.

There were no defensive wounds, so this wasn't a battle, it was an execution. There were slightly more bodies than there were heads. Archaeologists are pretty sure that this was part of Boleslaus' purge.

Boleslaus was still wiping the blood off his lance when he was told that his wife had given birth to a son. So he called him Strachkvas, which means 'Dreadful Feast'. Then he got on with being cruel and the Bohemians started to get all nostalgic for the days of Vaclav. Soon Vaclav was declared a saint, and then he was posthumously declared king by Otto the Great.

Then, five hundred years later, someone in Finland wrote a song about the coming of spring. It was a nice, bouncy tune with nice bouncy words, but it was Finnish and nobody noticed what a good melody it was until three hundred years after that, when an Englishman called John Mason Neale found the obscure Finnish tune and the obscure (in England) Bohemian saint and put the two together. Why the hell he did this, nobody really knows, but he did and it was published in 1853. Neale was an odd chap. He once wrote a history of church pews.

But somehow these carols work, and so do all the others. There's just something so timelessly English about 'Away in a Manger', 'O Little Town of Bethlehem' and 'We Three Kings', even though they're all American carols. There's something so Christmassy about Wenceslas and 'Ding Dong Merrily on High' and 'Jingle Bells' even though none of them mentions Christmas, and 'Jingle Bells' (which is also American) was written about Thanksgiving. A carol service is the only time when you can get hundreds of people singing together about important Christian truths like not abhorring the Virgin's womb, or insisting that Jesus was begotten, not created. There was once a thing called the Arian Heresy that insisted that Jesus was created, not begotten, and we still have to be terribly careful.

Carols of the carol service are a strange and beautiful weaving together of thoroughly different threads, and so are the readings.

The Bible

A book about Christmas probably ought to have something in it about Jesus's birth. Even though we may spend most of our time on trees and turkeys, everything, ultimately, must get back to the Bible, and the story we all think we know. It's from the New Testament that the whole thing springs, and only, actually, from a very few chapters.

Before I go any further I should point out that this book, astonishingly, will not provide you with the final answer as to whether God exists or not. I have checked several reliable reference works and none of them could say, not even the dictionary. I deal in trifles not truths, but I am aware that some people (particularly, for some reason, atheists) get very upset by the whole thing. They shout and hit people and send rude letters and weep. If you are one of these people, I suggest skipping a few pages ahead and starting the Santa Claus chapter. Santa is a truth that we can all agree on.

Still here? Splendid. There was once a fellow called Jesus of Nazareth who was nailed to a cross in about AD 33. All serious historians agree on that. The earliest Christian writings are the letters St Paul wrote in the 40s and 50s, but St Paul never once mentions the nativity or the Virgin birth; in fact, he seems to be unaware of them so he is Not Relevant to Our Purposes.

The first Gospel was Mark's, which was written some time in the late 60s. But Mark starts out with Jesus as a grown-up. There's no nativity or Virgin birth, so Mark too must be passed over. The last Gospel was John's, which was written in about AD 100 or shortly thereafter. John kind of sort of vaguely has a nativity insofar as he has the lovely opening section about the Word becoming flesh and dwelling amongst us. But that's it. Revelation was written in AD 95 and is utterly bewildering. It has no nativity.

The only two books with a nativity in are Matthew and Luke, which were probably written some time in the 80s or 90s. Let's start with Luke. It's the story we all know. Joseph and Mary are living in Nazareth when Mary becomes pregnant by the Holy

Spirit, but there's a census and they have to go to Bethlehem. When they get there, there's no room at the inn. So Mary gives birth in a stable and lays the baby Jesus in a manger. Then some shepherds who were abiding in the fields see an angel who tells them to go down to the stable. They do and everyone is much amazed. That's the Christmas story and we all know it well.

Now, Matthew. Mary and Joseph are living in Bethlehem. In a house. Mary then becomes pregnant by the Holy Spirit. She gives birth. Then some Magi come from the East. Matthew, incidentally, never says how many Magi, but he does say that they brought three gifts of gold, frankincense and myrrh, and so people always think there are three Magi. Anyway, the Magi stop off in Jerusalem and ask King Herod where the Messiah will be born and Herod tells them to have a look in Bethlehem and report back. The Magi go to Bethlehem, find the house and hand over the gifts; but they're warned in a dream not to report back to Herod, so they don't. Herod gets angry and orders that all the children of Bethlehem should be killed. Mary and Joseph are warned in a dream and flee to Egypt. Then they decide to come back to Judaea, but as Bethlehem is still too dangerous they move to Nazareth.

Those are the two stories. There's no manger in Matthew, no stable, no census and no shepherds. There is no star in Luke, no Magi, no myrrh and no flight to Egypt. The way to remember the difference is that Luke is the poor man's gospel. Shepherds were poor. Moreover, when they were out abiding in the fields all night they weren't able to do any of the ritual washing that a devout first-century Jew was supposed to do, so they were unclean. Luke's Jesus comes for the poor, the oppressed, those who sleep in stables and fields, and those who have failed to make hotel reservations.

Matthew's is the grand gospel. The second his Jesus is born, the very stars in the sky change. Gentiles arrive, kings are concerned, there's international travel and massacres. As I say, I am not here to answer questions of religion. But if you can't find truth in both these stories, you may be looking for the Wrong Sort of Truth.

It is surprising how few people notice these differences, although it may have something to do with the thousand nativity scenes we've all seen with the Magi and the shepherds standing side by side, Jesus in His manger and the star hanging above the stable. Each story is read out at the carol service and, like the carols themselves, the elements just blend together in our minds. It may be something to do with Edward White Benson's skill in laying out the carol service, or it may be the eggnog.

And now it is time to leave the church. It is Christmas Eve, and as you hurry home through the silent, holy night, somewhere in the far north a funny-looking Turkish chap is attaching reins to his reindeer.

5. *Santa Claus: The Biography*

Santa Claus is, without very much doubt, the most famous Turkish one-thousand-eight-hundred-year-old. Not that there's that much competition. He was born in the town of Patara in AD 270, or thereabouts, and it was clear right from day one that little Nicholas was a curious child. Back in those days, priests were meant to fast on Wednesdays and Fridays, and on Wednesdays and Fridays the new-born Nicholas *refused to breast-feed*.

Now, you may be wondering, dear reader, how a new-born baby would know which day of the week it was, or what the rules were for fasting priests. And so I should concede right now that the earliest biography of him was written four hundred years after his death, and there are scholars who doubt its accuracy. Indeed, there are a small number who think Nicholas may never have existed at all. But this is a minority position. Most historians believe in the existence of Santa Claus, just not the breast-feeding stuff.

With that in mind, I shall add that a later biography says that at his baptism, when he was still only a few days old, he stood, unsupported, on the altar for three hours to signify his devotion to the Trinity, and that when he did breast-feed he only ever suckled from his mother's right breast, to signify his intention to stand at God's right hand. Though I rarely lactate myself, I have checked with a few mothers of my acquaintance and they all agree that this would be absolute agony.

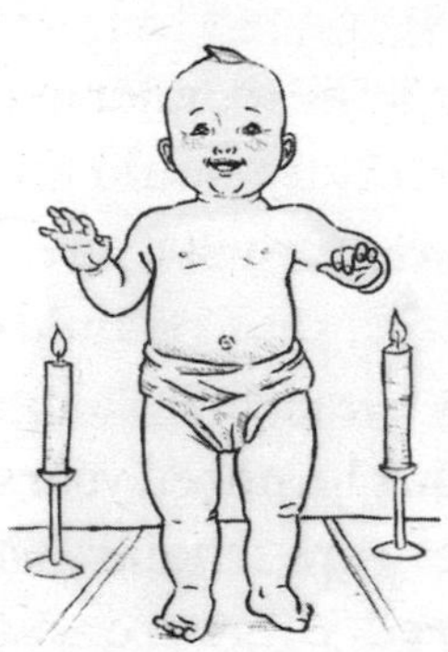

When Nicholas grew up he despised women, and drinking, and going to the theatre; and thus:

> *He preserved unquenched the lamp of his virginity, maintaining its fullness especially with the oil of charity.*

Which is rather surprising, because one thing all the biographies agree on is that he smelled fantastic. He exuded sweet odours and his breath was great. He smelled so good in fact that he was made the patron saint of perfumiers.

But I digress. Nicholas smelled so great that they made him Bishop of Myra, Myra being a city in southern Turkey that was named after the myrrh that grew in the mountains nearby (myrrh is a kind of aromatic resin you can get from trees). Nicholas was an only child, so when his parents died, he inherited all their money. But as he didn't like women, or drinking or going to the theatre, he had nothing to spend it on. So he turned to charity, the last refuge of the rich. And that's where you get the famous story, the one that started the whole legend and leads directly down the chimney of history to the fireplace of fame. It's a beautiful and touching and sentimental story and it goes like this:

> *There was a certain man among those who were recently famous and well-born, and he was a neighbour, his home being next to Nicholas'. Owing to the plotting and envy of Satan, who always has a grudge against those who prefer to live a life in accord with God, this man was squeezed by great poverty and lack of resources. He had gone from being well-off to extreme indigence. He had three daughters who were both shapely and very attractive to the eye, and he was willing to station them in a brothel so that he might thereby acquire the necessities of life for himself and his household. For no man among the lordly or powerful designed to marry them lawfully, and even among the lower-classes and those who owned the least bit*

of something there was no one well-minded enough to do this. And so the man looked away from his salvation and, as it were, fainted at the thought of prevailing upon God with persistence and prayer. By this logic he came to assent to situating his daughters in the abyss of such dishonour.

What's beautiful about that story is that it's something we can all relate to. It's a universal story that any parent will recognize. But Bishop Nicholas was a nosy neighbour, and he was having none of it. So he decided to give the chap some money for the dowry. But he was a modest man, so rather than knocking on the door he decided to throw the money in through his neighbour's window in the middle of the night. On the third night his neighbour caught him at it, but Nicholas made him swear that he would never tell a soul. His neighbour swore a solemn oath, and so it's a little surprising that we know the story at all.

What's important is that Nicholas became, unofficially, the patron saint of people in financial difficulties and, officially, the patron saint of pawnbrokers, who, to this day, hang three balls outside their shops in memory of the three gifts of Nicholas of Myra.

He did some other miracles, of course: he saved three sailors from drowning (and thus became the patron saint of sailors), he saved three soldiers who had been wrongly accused and he resurrected three boys who had been killed by an unscrupulous butcher. In fact, he liked to do everything in threes. I've no idea why.

And then St Nicholas died, as we all do, but he still smelled fantastic. In fact, some sort of stuff oozed out of his coffin and pilgrims would come hundreds of miles to get a bit of it. Allegedly, the date of his death was 6 December 343. Anyhow, that's his saint's day.

Whether he was declared a saint during his lifetime or afterwards we don't know. But St Nicholas of Myra he became, and it was after his death that his popularity really took off. You can get a rough idea of how popular a saint is by counting how many churches are dedicated to him. By the medieval period Nicholas was the most popular saint not mentioned in the Bible. In England alone there were 800 churches named after Nicholas.

And he was made patron saint of everything. Or practically everything. Children, repentant thieves, sailors, bargemen and bootblacks, drapers and druggists, grocers and grooms, lawyers and lovers, oil-merchants and orphans, merchants and murderers. In all, he's patron saint of over a hundred professions

(I don't know if you count murderer as a profession, but I do), eight countries and innumerable towns. He made the name Nicholas popular across Europe, as surname and first name and in all sorts of different forms. Some of these are obvious – like Nicola or Nixon; some a little less so – like Klaus and Nils; and some thoroughly obscure – like Cole, Collins and Nietzsche. All are named after the man from Myra.

People flocked to his tomb, and then in 1087, a bunch of Italian sailors flocked to his tomb, grabbed it and ran off back to Italy. They translated Nicholas' body (saints, for some reason, are never transported, they are translated) to Bari in southern Italy. The sailors claimed that they had taken the body because Myra had fallen to the Seljuk Turks and they were worried about him. But really, it was a tourism thing. Whichever town had the saint's body had a massive trade in pilgrims coming to sniff him. So they built a magnificent crypt to keep his bones in, and the Pope himself placed them there and blessed them. Then they built a church on top, and there he remains to this day. So, if you have a spoilt child who's bored with Santa's grotto, you can take them to visit Santa's grave.

And the strange, sweet-smelling stuff still drips from the casket. It's actually something of a scientific mystery. It used to be called manna, or oil. But it's been tested and it's basically pure water. What's weird is that there's no water going into the casket, so how does it come out? There are a bunch of theories – some miraculous and mad, some scientific and spoilsport – but nobody's really sure, and though I wrote them a friendly postcard asking to experiment, I have received no reply. The stuff comes out, on average 50ml per year,* and is collected up on 9 May, the anniversary of his translation.

And still his cult was spreading. People wrote plays about him, which were performed on his saint's day (see Chapter 2).

* That's about the same as a double whisky in a pub, not counting the ice.

In these he frees the innocents and helps fight the crusades, which is a little anachronistic, but who cares? And, because he was the patron saint of children and anonymous gifts, the custom began of giving children little gifts on 6 December, his saint's/death day, and saying that St Nicholas had brought them. This was definitely going on by the twelfth century in France. Usually, the children would have to leave their shoes out overnight, and if they had been naughty, they got nothing.

This tradition existed in lots of places. But for our purposes it's important that it existed in Holland, where St Nicholas was known as Sinta Klaas. Then the Reformation happened and Holland became Protestant. Protestants and Puritans hate saints (hagiophobia) because they think that Catholics worship them when they should be worshipping God. But they particularly hate saints who aren't mentioned in the Bible and might never have existed and are the subject of all sorts of stories about unlikely breast-feeding.

St Nicholas fulfilled all of these criteria,

so the Protestants tried to ban him. In Amsterdam they even made it a crime to hang around the city on St Nicholas' Eve carrying food. But they couldn't kill Sinta Klaas. Other saints perished, but Nicholas persisted. He had, after all, been patron saint of Amsterdam, and of sailors, and would therefore have been doubly patron of the sailors who set out from Old Amsterdam in 1624. They arrived at a little-known place called Manhattan Island and formally purchased it from the natives. The price paid was not a string of beads, but sixty guilders' worth of European merchandise, which is about £750 in today's money. They had founded New Amsterdam, the place where Sinta Klaas would become famous, because Santa may have been born in Turkey, but he's really a New Yorker.

Santa Claus in New York

America was founded on the principle that Christmas doesn't exist. You may hear other theories about religious freedom or colonial idealism or liberty or exploration, or other airy-fairy codswallop. But these fail to look at the cold, hard facts of the cold, hard Pilgrim Fathers who landed at Plymouth Rock. They were Puritans and Puritans hated Christmas. So they spent Christmas Day 1620 building the first houses of their new colony. Just to be utterly clear, they didn't do this for luck or love of Christmas, they did it because they didn't believe in Christmas at all and believed it should be an ordinary workday like any other. You can theorize all you like about colonialism and capitalism and the great unmapped continent, but when it comes to nails in wood, America was founded on the principle that Christmas doesn't exist.

It did next year. A little. A bunch of new, less puritan settlers arrived in early December on a ship called the *Fortune*. And when Christmas Day came round they told Governor Bradford that they couldn't, in all conscience, work on a holy day. The governor reluctantly agreed that they could have the day off. The original *Mayflower* pilgrims went out to work in the fields as usual, but when they got home for dinner they discovered the newcomers playing at stool-ball (an early form of cricket) and actually having fun. In public. This was too much for Governor Bradford and he confiscated their toys and ordered them indoors. He later noted with satisfaction that, since then, 'nothing hath been attempted that way, at least openly'.

But the new pilgrims kept coming, and many of them couldn't wait to celebrate. On one ship, the *Ark*, that came over to Maryland in 1633, Christmas Day fell while they were still at sea, and they got so drunk that 'about a dozen died'.

Of course, the Puritans tried to hold out against the relentless waves of fun that rolled across the Atlantic. They condemned and castigated, but that was only because there was so much fun to condemn. Cotton Mather, who was an eminent Bostonian author and preacher and scientist and the like, asked: 'Can you in your consciences think that our holy saviour is honoured by mirth, by long eating, by hard drinking, by lewd gaming, by rude revelling, by a mass fit for none but a Saturn or a Bacchus, or the light of Mahametan Romandon?'

Christmas was formally banned in several states and then unbanned under pressure from the British authorities and then banned again and then semi-banned. So, for example, in 1659 Massachusetts passed a law that 'anybody who is found observing, by abstinence from labour, feasting, or any other way, any such days as Christmas day, shall pay for every such offence five shillings'. It was repealed in 1681 under pressure from the British; and that was the usual way of it: the Americans hated Christmas, and it was the colonial authorities who forced them to tolerate it.

So it's rather odd that the rise of Santa Claus in America is actually down to anti-British feeling and American patriotism. Because in the American War of Independence, Santa was on the side of the Americans.

The Battle of the Saints

According to serious historians, there are various causes of the American Revolution involving tea and taxation, but the one that interests us is dancing. The British colonial authorities held balls. The English had one on St George's Day, the Scots on St Andrew's and the Irish and Welsh on St Patrick's and St David's. These were lavish affairs and in the run-up to the revolution they became something of a symbol of the powers that were. So American patriots started to mutter and mock and then set up their own saint's societies. The most famous of these is the Sons of St Tammany. Tammany wasn't a saint at all, he was a Red Indian chieftain, but that was the idea – to bait the British. They even had a St Tammany's Day on 1 May.

In New York the New Yorkers noticed that they had once been New Amsterdam until the British had invaded in 1664 and cruelly renamed their little city. So, in a nod to their Dutch heritage, they founded the Sons of St Nicholas in 1773. Again, this was part joke and part Brit-baiting, but it brought St Nick into the American Revolution on the American side. It is unknown how militarily effective St Nicholas was. He had, after all, been dead for 1,400 years, but he seems to have had a great effect on one actual New York soldier called John Pintard.

He did more for St Nicholas than St Nicholas ever did.

The Enthusiast

John Pintard was a classic busybody. He was rich, he was educated, he served as alderman to the City of New York, and had a mania for founding things and running things and instituting things. He founded the New-York Historical Society and the Massachusetts Historical Society; he was Sagamore of the Tammany Society; he was head of his Masonic lodge; he campaigned to have the Fourth of July and Washington's birthday made national holidays. But what he really loved was St Nicholas.

He tried very hard to have Nicholas of Myra declared patron saint of New York, and when he failed at that he made him patron saint of the Historical Society. He tried to get St Nicholas' Day recognized as a public holiday, but didn't manage it. But he never gave up. He, of course, gave his children gifts on St Nicholas' Day. One year he even made a life-size model of Santa Claus. Then he got his children to stand at one end of the nursery, opened the door at the other and used a pulley system so that the effigy would emerge above the door and his children could glimpse Santa Claus. His son 'immediately screamed out that it was his dear departed little brother'.

The Satirist

Washington Irving was born in the week that the American Revolution ended, hence his first name. He was a New Yorker from a well-to-do family and he had a talent for comedy. He's responsible for a baseball team, ladies' underwear, Batman and Santa Claus.

Let's start with Batman. Once upon a time there were some goats in a field in Nottinghamshire. This field became known as Goat-Farm or, in Old English, Gat-Ham, and eventually the name settled down as Gotham. The village is there to this day, just off the A453.

> *. . . some of the inhabitants engaged in endeavouring to drown an eel in a pool of water; some were employed in dragging carts upon a large barn, to shade the wood from the sun; others were tumbling their cheeses down a hill, that they might find their way to Nottingham for sale; and some were employed in hedging in a*

> *cuckoo which had perched upon an old bush which stood where the present one now stands.*

This may all have been a subtle ruse, because madness was once considered contagious. So the people of Gotham just wanted to be left alone. But, either way, Gotham became a byword for foolishness, and the people of Gotham became a byword for fools.

Fast forward a few centuries to New York and Washington Irving had, with some friends, set up a magazine called *Salmagundi* whose sole purpose was to make fun of New Yorkers. It was in issue number 17 that Irving first referred to New York as Gotham City, and thus started a tradition that continues to this day and morphed into the setting of the Batman comics and films.

The next year, though, Irving came up with a bigger and better plan to make fun of New Yorkers. He decided to satirize the New-York Historical Society (founder J. Pintard) by writing a spoof history of

New York. He would parody all their antiquarian waffling and romanticized scholarly nonsense. In order to make fun of the society, he joined it. So on St Nicholas' Day of that year he was at the annual dinner drinking a toast to the society's patron saint, and taking mental notes.

Irving wrote *A History of New-York from the Beginning of the World to the End of the Dutch Dynasty* very, very fast. But he planned its publication in minute detail. He put signs up around New York announcing that an elderly Dutchman called Diedrich Knickerbocker had gone missing from his hotel room. Then he pretended to be the hotel proprietor. He took out a newspaper advertisement announcing that Knickerbocker had not paid his bill and that all he had left behind was a large manuscript. If Knickerbocker didn't come back with the money, he would be forced to publish it himself to defray the costs. Of course, Knickerbocker didn't exist. Irving had got the name from a friend of his called Herman Knickerbocker who represented

New York in Congress. It sounded good and Dutch and that was good enough for Irving, because his book was all about the Dutch origins of New York and the importance of St Nicholas. He has St Nicholas directing the sailors, appearing in visions. He has a St Nicholas as the figurehead on the first boat to arrive in Manhattan. He has St Nicholas everywhere *just to make fun of Pintard*.

The book was an instant classic. America was a young country and it didn't really have its own literature yet. Irving, as a first-rate satirist who's pretty much as good as Sterne or Swift, fulfilled a need. It sold like hot cakes. It made him famous. It made the name Knickerbocker synonymous with New York, so much so that the New York Knicks derive their name straight from Irving's bestseller.

It was even wildly successful over in Britain. The British editions had illustrations by George Cruikshank that made fun of the funny Dutch trousers (Irving found Dutch national dress amusing). As a result, these became known as knickerbockers, and as a result of that a euphemism for ladies' underwear emerged in Britain: knickers.

You might imagine that being satirized in a national bestseller would dull your enthusiasm for things. But that, dear reader, is the difference between you and Pintard. I should make clear here that *A History of New-York . . .* is not vicious satire, it's very, very gentle. The great Russian writer Bulgakov once said that you should only satirize the things that you love. And I think Irving truly loved the New-York Historical Society. He certainly kept his membership.

And Pintard kept on campaigning for St Nicholas. The very next year, with a nation still laughing at him, he released a pamphlet with a poem in praise of St Nicholas, the giver of gifts. Above it is a picture of the stern-looking bishop, and next to him there are two boots hanging by a fireplace. The Dutch tradition had always involved boots. But these ones look a little saggy, a little like stockings.

At this point the bauble was back in Washington Irving's court. He had made fun of Pintard, it had been a bestseller, and Pintard was still going. So Irving doubled down. He brought out a second, revised edition of *A History of New-York*, in which he made even more ludicrous claims about Santa Claus.

So still writing in the persona of an eccentric historian, he added the lines:

> *At this early period was instituted that pious ceremony, still religiously observed in all our ancient families of the right breed, of hanging up a stocking in the chimney on St. Nicholas' Eve; which stocking is always found in the morning miraculously filled; for the good St. Nicholas has ever been a great giver of gifts, particularly to children.*

That is the first ever reference to Christmas stockings, and it's a joke, a joke making fun of John Pintard.

> *And the sage Oloffe dreamed a dream – and, lo! the good St. Nicholas came riding over the tops of the trees, in that self-same*

> *wagon wherein he brings his yearly presents to children.*

That is the first ever reference to Santa's mode of transport, and it's a joke, a joke making fun of John Pintard.

> *. . . in these degenerate days of iron and brass he never shows us the light of his countenance, nor ever visits us, save one night in the year; when he rattles down the chimneys of the descendants of the patriarchs, confining his presents merely to the children, in token of the degeneracy of the parents.*

That is the first ever reference to Santa's coming down the chimney, and it's a joke, a joke making fun of John Pintard. It was never, ever meant to be taken seriously.

It was immediately taken seriously.

New Yorkers loved the second edition as much as they loved the first. From then on, in New York, Santa Claus would fly around delivering presents down chimneys and placing them in stockings hung by the fireplace. And here is the beautiful paradox: Pintard won. By letting himself be satirized by blithely continuing with his campaign, he placed Santa Claus right at the heart of New York. Irving had joked and joked, but from now on his jokes would be told to children as the truth.

And Santa Claus was not quite complete. He still delivered his presents on St Nicholas' Eve, 5 December, and his wagon was drawn by horses and not by reindeer.

The Reindeer

Nobody really knows how Santa got his reindeer. The Dutch always believed that

Sinta Klaas lived (and still lives) in Spain. Pintard had insisted to his children that Santa Claus was a Dutchman who crossed the Atlantic every year by boat. He had, as yet, nothing whatsoever to do with the North Pole. All we really know about the reindeer is that Santa acquired them in New York.

In 1821 an anonymous poem was published in a magazine called the *Children's Friend*, which was published on Broadway. There was nothing peculiar about this. Stories about St Nicholas had been popular for a decade by then. They already had their traditions, such as the horse-drawn sky-wagon. That's why it's so strange that the poem begins:

> *Old Santeclaus with much delight*
> *His reindeer drives this frosty night,*
> *O'er chimney-tops, and tracks of snow,*
> *To bring his yearly gifts to you.*

Why? There are no reindeer in New York. There are no reindeer anywhere near New York. They're an obscure animal native to the far north of Europe. But there the poem is, and it's illustrated, and Santa has one prancing reindeer that draws his sleigh. Not a wagon, a *sleigh*.

So Santa had his transport, but he was still delivering on the wrong day, on St Nicholas' Eve. So when did he start to arrive on the night before Christmas? To answer that we shall have to turn to a poem called ''Twas the Night Before Christmas'.

Clement Clarke Moore

''Twas the Night Before Christmas' isn't actually called ''Twas the Night Before Christmas', that's just the first line. Its proper title is 'A Visit from St Nicholas', and it was written by yet another member of the New-York Historical Society, a man called Clement Clarke Moore.

Moore owned a beautiful rural estate just outside New York called Chelsea. Then New York expanded, Chelsea was developed and Moore owned a section of the city called Chelsea and more money than he knew what to do with. So he founded a theological college and made himself professor. He wrote a huge dictionary of ancient Hebrew, but that is not what he's remembered for. He published a lot of poetry that he took very seriously, but that is not what he's remembered for because it's mostly drivel and has been out of print for over a century.* The only poem of his that remains in print is one that he never wanted in print: a little rhyme that he wrote for his children in 1822 that became the blueprint for the modern Santa.

The general gist of the poem (in case you haven't read it), is that a father is about to go to sleep on Christmas Eve when he hears something outside, goes to the

* It's really pretty terrible. Take these opening lines:

> *Ye sacred Sisters; not for you, this strain:*
> *You heed no minstrelsy of earth-strung lyre;*
> *The softest siren notes would sound in vain*
> *To ears impatient for the heavenly choir.*

window and sees a chap arriving on a miniature sleigh drawn by eight tiny flying reindeer.

I knew in a moment it must be St Nick.
More rapid than eagles his coursers they came,
And he whistled, and shouted, and call'd them by name:
'Now! Dasher, now! Dancer, now! Prancer and Vixen,
'On! Comet, on! Cupid, on! Donder and Blitzen.'

And that's where the names come from – made up from scratch by a professor of theology.

St Nick comes down the chimney and he's a jolly-looking elf with a smile and a pot belly and he smokes a pipe – a bit like Irving's Santa, but with a weight problem. The stockings are by the fireplace, just as Pintard said they should be:

And fill'd all the stockings; then turn'd with a jerk,

And laying his finger aside of his nose
And giving a nod, up the chimney he
rose.

That little detail of the finger beside the nose comes straight from Irving's *History of New-York*:

And when St. Nicholas had smoked his pipe, he twisted it in his hat-band, and laying his finger beside his nose, gave the astonished Van Kortlandt a very significant look . . .

But Moore had made changes. First, he'd made it Christmas Eve, and second Santa is nice. Up until this point there had always been two sides to Santa. He brings presents for good children, for bad children he brings a cane that they can be beaten with. But not this time.

But I heard him exclaim, ere he drove out of
sight –
'Happy Christmas to all, and to all a good
night.'

There's no mention of a cane, no mention of bad children. In 1822 Santa decided that everyone should have a happy Christmas.

Clement Clarke Moore didn't seem to like his own poem very much. It was published anonymously, and became an instant hit. It was printed and reprinted and reprinted in innumerable magazines every year for decades, until Moore finally admitted to writing it and included it in his collected poems. Moore said that he'd got a lot of the ideas from his Dutch gardener, but nobody is sure if that's true.

Finding a Home

For a long time nobody seemed sure of Santa's address. Sometimes he lived in Spain, sometimes in Holland or Germany. Usually he was just in an anonymous house on an anonymous street in some town or other. But in 1869 he finally moved to the North Pole, which must have been a relief for the reindeer.

The move is documented in an incredibly

tedious poem called 'Santa Claus and His Works' by a chap called George Webster. But though the poem is awful, the pictures were wonderful, and that's what really counts in a children's book. The idea didn't catch on instantly – in 1875 Mark Twain was still telling his daughter that Santa lived in the Palace of St Nicholas on the Moon.

Santa needed a permanent address, not just for the sake of the elves and the reindeer, but because of the postal system. It's at this time that children started to write letters to Santa Claus. The letters had to have an address on them, and soon everyone agreed that that address should be the North Pole.

And then everyone started to disagree again. Just as St Nicholas' original body had been moved to boost the tourist trade, so, today, Greenland, Finland, the town of North Pole in New York State, and the town of North Pole in Alaska, all compete to be the True Home of Santa. It's all about the tourism. I have visited none of these places, but if I could I would go to Rovaniemi, Finland, where, as part of the Santa Experience, you can eat reindeer.

Santa Turns Cannibal

One day, Santa Claus came to England and ate Father Christmas. That may sound rather odd, but you have to remember that Father Christmas is a completely different person from Santa, or at least he was until he got eaten.

Father Christmas was an Englishman. He was first mentioned in a hymn from the late fourteenth century and from then on he pops up here and there. But Father Christmas did not have reindeer or sneak into your house at night to inspect your stockings. He was merely a personification of the Christmas season.

Just as Jack Frost is cold weather, Uncle Sam is the USA or Death is death; so Father Christmas was simply an allegorical figure. He stood for Christmas. So, when English people wanted to depict him, they did so however they liked. They could even give him other names. Here he is introducing himself in a masque* from 1634:

> *Christmas, old Christmas? Christmas of London, and Captain Christmas? . . . they would not let me in: I must come another time! A good jest, as if I could come more than once a year; why, I am no dangerous person, and so I told my friends o' the Guard. I am old Gregory Christmas still, and though I come out of Popes-Head-Alley as good a Protestant, as any in my Parish . . .*

The reason for that last bit is the old suspicion that Christmas is all Catholic claptrap. And indeed, twenty years later, the Puritans banned Christmas in England. Everybody reacted by rioting and writing satirical pamphlets (possibly at the same time). These pamphlets had snappy, memorable titles like:

* A masque was like a play, but boring.

> *THE ARRAIGNMENT Conviction and Imprisonment of CHRISTMAS On S. Thomas Day last, And How he broke out of Prison in the Holidayes and got away, onely left his hoary hair, and gray beard, sticking between two Iron Bars of a Window. With An Hue and Cry after CHRISTMAS, and a Letter from Mr. Woodcock, a Fellow in Oxford, to a Malignant Lady in LONDON. And divers passages between the Lady and the Cryer, about Old Christmas: And what shift he was fain to make to save his life, and great stir to fetch him back again. With divers other Witty Passages. Printed by Simon Minc'd Pye, for Cissely Plum-Porridge; And are to be sold by Ralph Fidler, Chandler, at the signe of the Pack of Cards in Mustard-Alley, in Brawn Street. 1645.*

But they also have good standard descriptions of Gregory Christmas. He was an old man with a white beard (because Christmas is old) and he was fat and jolly (because Christmas involved a lot of food and drink). One description even says that he was sexy:

> *The wanton Women dote after him; he helped them to so many new Gownes, Hatts, and Hankerches, and other fine knacks, of which he hath a pack on his back, in which is good store of all sorts, besides the fine knacks that he got out of their husbands' pockets for household provisions for him.*

But that is the only reference I have ever been able to find to Father Christmas giving presents. And it probably doesn't refer to Christmas presents, because English people almost never gave presents on Christmas Day, they gave presents on New Year's Day, until Santa came to town.

The American Santa Claus arrived in England sometime in the 1860s, and promptly ate poor Gregory C. Santa was exported by America with all of their Christmas traditions in the form of books and stories and pictures. Oddly enough, I *think* that this was America's first great cultural export. These days, after a hundred years of jazz, Hollywood, rock'n'roll and cheeseburgers, we are used to the idea of the USA as the cultural hegemon. But back in the nineteenth century it was Britain in cultural control. Until Santa struck back.

One of Charles Dickens's daughters recalled how, when she was growing up in the 1840s, they had been taken out to a toyshop on Christmas Eve and allowed to choose one small item. But on New Year's Eve the house was piled high with presents, which they could open at precisely midnight. By the 1860s all that had changed.

Santa now came to English houses too, and, as in America, he came on Christmas Eve.

And poor old Father Christmas? Well, the English kept his name, but nothing else. But we did, very quickly, add one thing more: we took Santa shopping. The first Santa's grotto was unveiled at the J. P. Roberts department store in east London in 1888. And oddly enough a department store is where Santa acquired his final companion.

Coca-Cola

Something brief ought to be said here about the idea that Coca-Cola created the Santa Claus we know and dressed him in red and white. They didn't. It's as simple as that. Even if you were to limit your study purely to the advertising campaigns of American soft drink manufacturers, Coca-Cola still didn't dress Santa in red and white. White Rock ginger ale had Santa exactly as he is today in a campaign that started in 1923, ten years before Coke started using him. But Santa had been red and white for ages. You can see it in nineteenth-century depictions, including those of Thomas Nast. You can even find him wearing red with a white fur trim in a painting of 1837, which was commissioned by the New-York Historical Society. That is that.

Rudolph

Santa snowballs. Any writer can add any detail to his life. Some stick, some do not. In 1850 Louisa May Alcott wrote about his elves in a short story. They stuck. In the late nineteenth century there were various references to his wife, and she still pops up now and again, though it doesn't seem to be a very stable or happy relationship. But the most successful addition to the scene came from a simple marketing ploy.

Montgomery Ward department store in Chicago used to run a Christmas promotion where customers were given a free colouring book with each purchase. They had always bought the colouring books in, but in

1939 they decided to make their own, and they sent one of their copywriters off to write a story.

His name was Robert L. May and his brief was to produce a story vaguely involving Christmas and an animal. That Robert L. May was Jewish doesn't seem to have bothered anybody. May set to work and wrote a story in verse, and it's worthwhile explaining it here as most people only know the song, which is rather different.

It's about Rudolph, an ordinary reindeer who *doesn't* live at the North Pole. He lives in (and I hesitate to write this) an ordinary reindeer village. He is, however, very unpopular with the other little reindeer on account of his incandescent nose. This renders Rudolph miserable, but he cheers himself up with the thought that Christmas is coming and that Santa will present him with presents.

However, Santa has a problem. It's a very foggy Christmas Eve and he has trouble finding his way, which slows him down. It looks as though he's not going to get all his presents delivered in one night. But then, as he creeps into a child's room in an ordinary reindeer village, he notices a glow glimmering from the bed. He wakes Rudolph up and asks if he will act as a living fog-light. Rudolph agrees, and with the new-found illumination Santa just manages to complete his round by sunrise. He then returns to the village where all of the other reindeer see Rudolph landing with the eight superstars of the reindeerish world, and they're all very impressed.

The book was an instant hit and quickly became a bestseller in its own right; and six years later May's brother-in-law wrote a song based upon it. From then on Santa had nine reindeer.

There is, though, a much better and more scientific theory for why Rudolph was teased by the other reindeer. You see, Rudolph is transsexual. Rudolph in all the original illustrations has horns at Christmas. Male reindeers shed their horns during the winter. Rudolph, right from the earliest depictions in the Montgomery Ward colouring book, has a full set of antlers. Rudolph is female.

The End

And that is the story of how a stern and serious saint from third-century Turkey ended up as a jolly fat man delivering presents from the North Pole, and why we leave some food and drink out for St Nicholas of Myra, as food and drink is the heart of Christmas. Indeed, you can write its history in calories.

6. *Christmas Dinner*

Christmas Day is when we celebrate the great mystery of the incarnation of Our Lord by eating an awful lot of meat. This is somehow appropriate because 'incarnation' and 'carnivore' are etymologically almost the same. They both come from the Latin word *carnis*, meaning flesh. One means 'into flesh' (the Word became flesh and dwelt amongst us and we have beheld its glory), and the other means 'flesh eating'. It's also the root of 'carnal' and of 'charnel', because a charnel house is filled with dead, fleshy bodies.

So why all this meat? Well, first there's much less meat at Christmas now than there used to be, and secondly 'tis the season to eat meat. God made it that way, at least in Europe; presumably God had other plans for

Australia (though nobody has yet worked out what those plans are).*

Once upon a time, everybody worked on a farm.† In summer they made hay while the sun shone. At harvest time they reaped what they had sown. Then they watched their flocks in the fields up until November. From

* I'm afraid that I've rather neglected the Australian Christmas in this book. Indeed, if I recall correctly, back in the Preface I implied that Christmas and Midsummer were the opposite ends of the year, which is bound to raise antipodean hackles and heckles. The problem is that, as the *Australian Christmas Collection* of 1886 observed, 'The native Australian lives in a sunny land, inhales a balmy air, and gazes on cheerful skies. His parents' conception of a genuine Christmas is far different to his. Their recollections [. . .] are associated with bleak winds and wintry storms [. . .] Your native Australian cannot understand or appreciate such a Christmas.' Instead they spend it in 'healthful excursions' and 'boating expeditions'.

† All facts in this chapter are going to be a little bit generalized.

this point on there isn't really enough grass growing, so they took them back to the barn and fed them the hay. Not all of them. Hay is a valuable commodity, so mid-November was the time when you decided which animals you were going to feed all winter, and which you were going to kill today. As the old saying goes about Halloween:

At Hallowtide slaughter time entreth in
And then doth the husbandmen's feasting begin.

Where a husbandman is just a farmer. From then on, there wasn't really that much for a husbandman to do. The grain was in the granary. The flocks were in the barn. So, how do you pass the time? Hunting. There are still a lot of birds around and people used to eat many more birds than we do now. Larks, woodcocks, plovers. It was once traditional to hunt wrens on Boxing Day. In fact, the only birds that we in Britain absolutely never hunted were robins. It has always been bad luck to kill a robin, hence the nursery rhyme. Hence also evolution.

Robins on the Continent are very shy birds, robins in Britain are notoriously unafraid of humans and tend to bother us when we're doing the gardening. So far as anyone can tell (and this is impossible to prove), that's because robins were hunted everywhere else, and this aggressive form of natural selection led to different behaviours.

Incidentally, the reason that the robin has a red breast is (and this is less scientifically certain) that at the nativity Mary was shivering in the stable and the little fire she had to keep her warm was going out. But then a friendly robin saw her distress and came and hovered above the fire, fanning its flames and keeping the infant Jesus warm. The fire burnt the robin's breast red, and it has remained so to this day. Or that's the story.

But the rule was, if it's not a robin you can kill it, and as a rule you did. December was an avian massacre. There's a Christmas recipe from 1747 for a large turkey stuffed with a whole goose stuffed with a chicken stuffed with a pigeon stuffed with a partridge, like a Russian doll made of meat. Does that remind you of anything? A song maybe? A Christmas song? A Christmas song listing birds largest to smallest ending with a partridge? That was first published in 1780?

On the seventh day of Christmas my true
love sent to me:
Seven swans a-swimming,
Six geese a-laying,
Five gold rings,
Four calling birds,
Three French hens,
Two turtle doves,
And a partridge in a pear tree.

But . . . (I hear you wail) but what about the five gold rings? Well, the 'gold rings' are almost certainly ring-necked pheasants, or ring pheasants, as they used to be called. Thc 'gold'

would be the colour of the wings, or perhaps the female plumage. Or the 'rings' could be ring-bills, ring-birds, ring-blackbirds, ring-buntings, ring-dotterels, ring-pigeons, ring-plovers, ring-sparrows or ring-thrushes. There's a veritable aviary of birds that could be called rings, and, given the context, it seems reasonable to make it a week of birds.

But . . . (I hear you moan) what about the pear tree? What's that doing there? Well, almost everyone who's studied the song agrees that the pear tree is probably a corruption of the French *perdrix*, which means 'partridge'. The song is, after all, probably of French origin as the British common partridge doesn't usually perch in trees at all, while the French red-legged partridge does.

It's not certain, of course, that the song is based on a recipe, but the fact that the birds are arranged largest to smallest makes it pretty damned likely.

So, to return to the history, if you were a traditional peasant at Christmas you had a larder full of meat and very little to do. It's a vegetarian's nightmare. Meat, which had been a luxury food all year, was now a drug on the market. There's a seventeenth-century book called *The Accomplish't Cook* that lays out quite clearly what you should serve for Christmas dinner:

A collar of brawn.
Stewed broth of mutton marrow bones.
A grand salad.
A pottage of caponets.
A breast of veal in a stoffado.
A boiled partridge.
A chine of beef, or sirloin roast.
Minced pies.
A jigot of mutton with anchovy sauce.
A made dish of sweetbread.
A swan roast.
A pasty of venison.
A kid with a pudding in his belly.
A steak pie.
A haunch of venison roasted.
A turkey roast and stuck with cloves.
A made dish of chicken in puff pastry.
Two brant geese roasted, one larded.
A custard.

And that's just the first course. The second course is rather bigger with quails, 'six tame pigeons' (why they should be tame baffles me, as they're dead), and a total of three turkeys. Meat was everywhere.

And what about the veg? Well, here things get a little complicated. The obvious answer is nuts. Lots of nuts, because nuts keep well and they're still a Christmas staple. But unfortunately there's very little fruit, only dried stuff, which is why – even in this age of aeroplanes – we have dried fruit at Christmas. Most of this had to be imported from Spain or other points south, and so, unlike meat, currants were a luxury food that only show-offs would buy. But most people are show-offs.

Several of these foods actually became popular (with the rich) during the Crusades, when people (who were rich) went off to fight in the Holy Land and acquired a taste for funny east Mediterranean foods. You can still see their origins in the names. Currants were once *raysyn of Curans*, from French *reisin de Corauntz*, because they were from Corinth. A sultana is technically the title of a sultan's wife, but was also a kind of raisin that grew in Turkey – a 'queen raisin', like a king cabbage. Plums dry well and can be put into a plum pudding, the forerunner of our Christmas pudding, which also contains raisins. Of course, these could only be bought by the rich, but the poor still got to eat the foods of the Orient.

Noblemen were supposed, on Christmas Day, to open up their houses to the poor, who could come and have a fantastic, meaty, slap-up meal. Probably the best meal they had all year. This may sound like a romantic rose-tinted idea of Ye Olde Christmas, but it's true and important. It was so important that James I banned the nobility from staying in London for Christmas. They had to go home to their manor houses and make nice and festive to the local villagers, because social cohesion was thought to depend on it.

The villagers themselves loved this time of year and would go around wassailing and

guizing. Wassailing means going to people's houses with a large bucket and demanding that they fill it with booze. Guizing is pretty much the same thing, but wearing masks. Guizing is short for disguising, and *guizer* is the origin of the Cockney term *geezer*. There was also a tradition about hitting apple trees that I don't understand. The whole thing was roughly like trick or treating. It was (a) great fun and (b) the one time of the year that the villagers could play at being equal with the nobility. Sometimes they were even in charge. Many noblemen would appoint a Lord of Misrule. This was a commoner who, for the twelve days of Christmas, got to be in charge of everything. He could order the noblemen and all their servants about and invent merry japes and force them to dance for him. Of course, any sensible Lord of Misrule actually knew which side his bread was buttered and made sure he was madcap in a non-threatening way. But that was, essentially, the point: the peasantry got to play at being nobles for one week of the year, and that made them much happier about not being nobles for the other fifty-one weeks. Karl Marx had a word for this, but I can't remember what it is.

So the Tudor Christmas was basically a great big twelve-day party when the poor got to eat well, the peasants got to play at being lords and everyone went on a semi-psychotic crusade against birdlife. And then – as so very, very often in this book – the Puritans happened.

Quite aside from violently shortening King Charles I, the Puritans banned Christmas. They actually did this by degrees. In 1642 they banned Christmas plays. In 1644 they noticed that Christmas Day was the last Wednesday* of the month, which was meant to be a fast day, so they declared that Christmas was still there, but you couldn't eat anything. They doubled down on this by insisting that Parliament meet on Christmas Day as it was a workday like any other.† Then in 1647 they declared that Christmas was a day of penance; and then in 1652 they just banned the whole thing.

People rioted. As government decisions go, banning Christmas is never going to win

* See also the Computist (Chapter 1) and St Nicholas of Myra (Chapter 5).

† See also the Pilgrim Fathers (Chapter 5).

you many votes. But mostly it was the poor that rioted because they wanted their Christmas meal, the one good meal they got all year from the house of the local landowner. James I had been right, Charles I had been wronged, and Christmas was officially illegal for the next eight years.

That didn't destroy Christmas utterly. It couldn't. Whenever Christmas is banned, in fact whenever anything is banned, it is only really banned in public. People could, and did, shut up shop for the day, stay home and eat a nice, meaty meal. But Christmas was hit hard. Cromwell himself noticed that:

> *. . . there was every wilful and strict observation of the day commonly called Christmas day throughout the Cities of London and Westminster by a general keeping of their shops shut up and that there were contemptuous speeches used by some in favour thereof, which the Council conceiving to be on the old grounds of superstition and malignancy and tending to the avowing of the same contempt of the*

> *present laws and government I have thought fit that the Parliament be moved to take the same into consideration for such further provisions and penalties for the abolishing and punishing of those old superstitions . . .*

Christmas was banned for nearly a decade until the Restoration of the monarchy in 1660. And though it survived it was damaged. It would never again be the glorious feast it had been in Tudor times, and ever after historians would write nostalgically of the good old days of Merrie Christmas in Olde England. And they weren't really wrong. Even Walter Scott, who was usually soppy about Scotland, would get soppy about the lost English Christmas:

> *England was merry England, when*
> *Old Christmas brought his sports again,*
> *'Twas Christmas broached the mightiest*
> *ale,*
> *'Twas Christmas told the merriest tale.*
> *A Christmas gambol oft could cheer*
> *The poor man's heart through half the year.*

Christmas limped onwards. It had a bit of a revival in the early eighteenth century, but then, one day, everybody decided to leave their farms and move to the city, thus causing the Industrial Revolution and Charles Dickens. This also killed Christmas.

Those Scrooges who are sickened when Christmas trees go up early, when Mariah Carey is singing in every shop and all around are cheerful children and angry adults, would have loved the early nineteenth century. In twenty out of the forty-five years from 1790 to 1835, *The Times* newspaper didn't mention Christmas at all.
Nothing. Nil.

The reason was structural. People worked in factories now and factories work just as well on 25 December as on any other day. The age of the lazy farmers was over. Moreover, in the city you couldn't do any of the proper Christmas things. When you live in a little village and some drunk chaps come to your front door wearing masks and demanding stuff, it's a bit of fun. In a city it's called Home Invasion Robbery.

People still had a meal, of course, but there weren't so many larks and swans in it. In 1823 a Frenchman observed: 'Probably there is not a single table spread on Christmas Day throughout the land – from the King's to the lowest artisan's that can scrape together enough to buy him a dinner at all – that is not furnished with roast beef and plum pudding.' But what about the larks and wrens?

And occasional people did try guizing in the city. In New York they had things called kalithumpian bands, which were basically a bunch of poor people marching through rich areas banging together pots and pans and blowing whistles, while the wealthy cowered indoors or hired security guards.

But after everyone had lived in the city for a while, they developed the nagging feeling that they had lost something. Victorian England was obsessed with the idea that it had gained the world but lost its roots. Where were the merry yeomen and the noble lords and the other stuff of yore? And, most particularly, where was Christmas? In 1836 Charles Dickens said:

'People will tell you that Christmas is not to them what it used to be.' And it wasn't.

So everyone had a sit down and a think and scratched their collective heads and realized that, though Christmas had always been about the village, now that there were no more villages it would be about the house, the home, the hearth and, most of all, the children. It might be possible to celebrate Christmas indoors. This was something of a revelation. Christmas could be about family, about sitting at home and eating one bit of really good meat: beef if you were poor, goose if you were mid-ranking, and turkey* if you could afford it.

I think, dear reader, that the inevitable time has come to say something about *A*

* The reason turkeys are called turkeys, even though they come from America, is that English people confused them with a completely different bird that was imported via Turkey from Madagascar. The French made a similar mistake and thought they were from India or *d'Inde*, or in modern French *dinde*. But I wrote about all of this in *The Etymologicon*.

Christmas Carol. First, because it sums up everything I've been saying here; and second, because anyone writing a history of Christmas is legally required to mention it. So, six quick points:

1. Scrooge represents everyone who works in the city, that's why it never actually says what job he does. You may think that he's a slum landlord or a money lender, but though there's one brief mention of a debt towards the end of the book, Dickens never, ever specifies. (If you're absolutely positive that you remember a specific trade, you're probably thinking of the film version with the Muppets.)
2. The opening scene has Scrooge complaining that he has to give Bob Cratchit the day off, thus 'picking a man's pocket every twenty-fifth of December!' Because unlike the old rural idyll in the yules of yore, city workers could work all year. Gone are the twelve days of idleness.

3. Then the Ghost of Christmas Past takes Scrooge back to his childhood in the countryside, because Scrooge is the archetypal Victorian with a rural past and an urban present.

4. When we go back in time to Fezziwig's party, when Scrooge was a young man, we find that Christmas used to be fun, but now it's not.

5. The Ghost of Christmas Present shows Scrooge that Bob Cratchit, who is poor, is planning to eat goose. He also shows him that all the good Christmases occur indoors. Whether it's the Cratchits or Scrooge's nephew or miners on the moor or lighthouse keepers (though I concede that lighthouse keepers can't very well spend it outside).

6. When Scrooge has changed his ways, the first thing he does is buy Bob Cratchit a turkey, because turkey is better and more expensive than goose.

It's probably also worth mentioning that there are no Christmas presents and no

Christmas tree and no Santa Claus because this is England in 1843 and none of those things had got popular yet.

There are also No Brussels Sprouts.

Brussels sprouts first appear in an English recipe book in 1845 in *Modern Cookery for Private Families* by Eliza Acton. They were meant to be buttered and eaten on toast. I have tried this and you shouldn't. Brussels sprouts divide opinion, but the main reason that they have become a Christmas food is that they grow in the winter, and that they actually taste better after a frost. For some strange biological reason, the ice sweetens them.

The 1840s also brought the Christmas cracker to a previously jokeless world. The cracker started off as a kind of novelty sweet. The sweet had a wrapper, which in and of itself was a novelty back in those dull days; the wrapper was a French invention and, when you think about it, is completely pointless, if a little pretty (I did say it was French). The novelty was the idea of putting a little strip of mild explosive into the sweet wrapper so that when you pulled at either end you got a little explosion. Cracker bonbons, as they were called, first appeared in 1841, and then in 1847 they were invented.

That chronology may seem a little odd to you, and it does to me, but a man called Thomas Smith absolutely insisted that he invented the Christmas cracker in 1847. He even has a lovely story about it. He was sitting by the fire thinking about sweet wrappers (he ran a cake shop), when all of a sudden the burning log emitted a loud *crack* and at that instant the idea came to him and . . .

He managed to invent something that had been around for *at least* six years. Cynics would say that this is implausible. Cynics would say that a guy who ran a cake shop probably knew about something that had been commonplace in his trade for years. For once, I am firmly with the cynics.

All Tom Smith really did was remove the sweet. Where once crackers had been full of food, they now contained a little strip of paper with a love poem or, later, a weak joke. What Tom Smith was definitely good at was marketing the things (and inventing stories about how he'd invented inventions). He made bonbon crackers into Christmas crackers.

In fact, he made bonbon crackers Christmas *cossaques* (named after the Russian soldiers and their guns), and then a few years later he made them Christmas crackers. But he was the first man to associate a novelty sweet with Christmas; and then he was the first man to realize that if a sweet wrapper is interesting enough, you don't even need the sweet. His son Walter had the idea of putting paper crowns inside and the company grew and grew and grew. Tom Smith Crackers remains, to this day, the largest manufacturer of Christmas crackers in the world.

Many strange things have been put in crackers, though to my knowledge no Grinch-like assassin has ever thought of hiding a bomb in one, which seems rather wasteful as there's already a detonator.

Once, in 1927, a young man sent an engagement ring to Tom Smith Crackers along with a ten-shilling note and a letter. He asked them to place the engagement ring inside a cracker so that he could propose to his beloved over Christmas dinner. It's all rather romantic, except he forgot to include his name or a return address. The ring remains in the company safe to this day.*

Once the crackers are cracked and the turkey's goose is cooked and everybody is thoroughly stuffed with stuffing, it is time for the Christmas pudding (those dried fruits that we know so well) and what *may just* be the most ancient Christmas tradition – the silver sixpence hidden deep in the deliciousness.

The shiny silver sixpence was first minted in England in 1551 and was produced for 400 years until 1947, when somebody decided it was too shiny and they

* You could probably claim it, if you could show that you were of age in 1927.

started making it out of cupronickel. But it is most famous as the lucky coin found hidden in the Christmas pudding. However, your belly at this point on Christmas Day and money through history have one thing in common: inflation. It used to be just a threepenny bit that was hidden away. And before that it was simply a bean.

But the bean, a few centuries ago, brought you much more than good luck. It brought you power. Whoever found the bean in the pudding was allowed to order everybody around for the rest of the day. They became the master of Christmas ceremonies. If they wanted you to dance, you had to dance. If they wanted you to sing, you had to sing. For the man who found the bean was the Bean King and everybody had to do as he said.

I say man, because there was also the Pea Queen. She was the female equivalent and each pudding contained one bean and one pea. What I can't work out here is how on earth you made sure that somebody of the right sex got the right bit. It's a little peculiar, but it definitely seems to have happened. Robert Herrick wrote a poem about it, and that's all the proof I need; because although Robert Herrick was the ugliest poet who ever lived, his poetry is beautiful.

Now, now the mirth comes
With the cake full of plums,
Where bean's the king of the sport here;
Beside, we must know
The pea also
Must revel as queen in the court here.

Begin then to choose,
This night, as ye use,
Who shall for the present delight here;
Be a king by the lot,
And who shall not
Be Twelve-day queen for the night here!

Which known, let us make
Joy-sops with the cake;
And let not a man then be seen here,
Who unurged will not drink,
To the base from the brink,
A health to the king and the queen here!

Next crown the bowl full
With gentle lamb's wool,
And sugar, nutmeg, and ginger,
With store of ale, too;
And this ye must do
To make the wassail a swinger.

Give then to the king
And queen, wassailing,
And though with ale ye be wet here,
Yet part ye from hence
As free from offence
As when ye innocent met here.

And before you object, swinger does rhyme with ginger, you see it's something that swinges, or goes off with a bang.

Herrick's Christmas* tradition goes straight back to an even earlier one. In case you've been skim-reading, I said a few pages ago that, around the beginning of December, Tudor nobles would appoint a

* Herrick is referring to Twelfth Night, but that's still the Christmas season, and this is part of his cycle of Christmas poems. So there.

lowly servant to be the Lord of Misrule. This guy was roughly the same as the Bean King, except that his rule lasted a month, and he had a budget. Indeed, he had a pretty big budget if he was the king's Lord of Misrule. He could organize dances, pranks, anything he liked. He could even imprison those who disobeyed him. And this tradition goes back to an even earlier one.

All over Europe, from the tenth century onwards, there were boy bishops. These did exactly what it says on the tin. They were boys, choirboys to be precise, who were made bishops for a month over Christmas. They got all the ceremonial clothes, they got the mitre, they got the lot. And they were also entitled to order around all of the adult priests who had been ordering them around all year. This must have been a rather odd time. The motto for educating choirboys back then was *quot verba, tot verbera*, which translates roughly as 'as many words as beatings', and now the masters were the servants. Boy bishops were so widespread that it's hard to make any proper generalizations about them. In some places they were the best and most well-behaved boys chosen by the schoolmasters. In others they were the worst, chosen by the boys. Some sources say that it was all a very holy and serious affair in which the Christ child was celebrated by a child bishop, in order to teach us deep and childish truths. Other sources say the opposite. As with all future odd relationships between choirboys and bishops, it is hard to get to the bottom of it.

The first evidence for boy bishops comes from the early tenth century, and it might just be based on an earlier practice. Throughout this book, from the Preface to this very moment at the end of Christmas dinner, I have been pooh-poohing the notion of pagan origins. This is simply because every time I have gone back to the primary sources the pagan origins have not been there. There is a curious school of thought among historians of Christmas that 'I don't know' equates to 'definitely pagan'; it would be an interesting methodology to use in a maths exam.

But I ought to throw pagans a crumb, I suppose. Despite a five-hundred-year gap, despite all the waves of barbarians and invaders that smashed across Europe in those centuries, despite the absolute lack of records or proof, it is just *possible* that the coin in your Christmas pudding goes all the way back to the Roman festival of Saturnalia.

I did not say probable.

Saturnalia lasted from 17 to 23 December and utterly central to the celebration was the *Saturnalicius princeps*, the King of Saturnalia. The princeps was elected by lot . . . well, to some extent. It's a tad suspicious that Nero just happened to win the lottery when he was a boy. But let that pass. A boy, or sometimes a lowborn adult, would be elected the King of Saturnalia. He would have absolute power to organize feasts and dancing and general japes. During Saturnalia masters served their servants, the normal order was reversed, and it was just (or sort of) like the boy bishops, the Lords of Misrule, the Bean King and the Pea Queen.

It's approximately the same thing. It's the right time of year. The theory is tenuous, but tenable. It is *just* possible that the coin in your Christmas pudding is the last survival of a two-thousand-year-old tradition. And in all my researches into Christmas traditions, that is the most convincing pagan origin I've found.

So, let us get back to the good old traditions. If you have found the coin, explain to everybody that they are now your servants. And then you'll have to give them a box, on Boxing Day.

7. *Boxing Day*

Once upon a time, there was a thing called a Christmas box. A Christmas box was a box with a small hole cut in it, like a piggy bank, through which coins could be dropped. It was kept in a church and, like a piggy bank, it could not be opened, only smashed. The smashing was done at Christmas, hence the name: Christmas box.

And then, like all Christian things at Christmas, the box was secularized. The first place that it's mentioned is in gambling dens, where customers were meant to leave a tip for the benefit of the butler in a box that was smashed open at Christmas. Then other places followed suit and soon every private house had a Christmas box for the servants. As one chap put it in 1634:

> *It is a shame, for a rich Christian to be like a Christmas boxe, that receives all, and nothing can be got out, till it be broken in peeces.*

And like any source of free money, the idea got taken up by others. What about those who served you, but who were not your servants? Every tradesman you dealt with could in some way consider himself your servant. They didn't want a box, they just wanted a large Christmas tip. Apprentices were especially interested in the custom. By the mid-eighteenth century the whole thing had got a trifle expensive. Sir John Fielding pointed out:

> *If you should send for a carpenter to drive a nail or two, or an upholder to take down a bed, a blacksmith to mend your poker, or a brick-layer to mend a hole in the wall, you will certainly see all their apprentices at Christmas, and add to these your baker, butcher, brewer, grocer, poulterer, fish-monger, tallow-chandler,*

> *glazier, corn-chandler, dustman, chimney-sweeper, watchman, beadles, lamp-lighters, not to forget the person who sells brick dust to your footman to clean his knives, and you will have some idea of the Christmas boxes of a private family.*

He then continued that the apprentices will only go and spend it on prostitutes who will give them syphilis and kill them. Yet still they came, every year on the first *weekday* after Christmas. Not on a Sunday, as that was their day off. And thus the first weekday after Christmas became known as Boxing Day. The beadles, it appears, were particularly persistent. Beadles were a sort of policeman paid for by the parish. In *The Pickwick Papers* Sam Weller is trying to write a love letter:

> *''Tain't in poetry, is it?' interposed his father.*
>
> *'No, no,' replied Sam.*
>
> *'Wery glad to hear it,' said Mr Weller. 'Poetry's unnat'ral; no man ever talked*

> *poetry 'cept a beadle on boxin'-day, or Warren's blackin', or Rowland's oil, or some of them low fellows; never you let yourself down to talk poetry, my boy.'*

But, despite what Mr Weller may think, the servants deserve their boxes. Christmas wasn't always the best time for them. There was a servant called Rose Armstrong in Preston in the early twentieth century and her Christmas was far from merry:

> *One Christmas I was at Longbridge and Christmas Day come and I was a bit homesick, you know, and had our Christmas Day's dinner. I washed up and all that, and she said, 'Has tha finished now?' I said, 'Yes, madam,' so she said, 'Well if thou get all the paper there, you'll see a lot of paper there and there's a big needle there and a ball of string, if you go down to the paddock, sit there and take the scissors and cut some paper up and thread it for the lavatory.' And I sat there on Christmas Day and I think I cried a bucketful of tears. Christmas afternoon*

and I was sat . . . sitting cutting bits of paper like that and getting this big needle, threading them and tying knots in them and tying them on these hoops . . . Sitting there on the lavatory seat.

Decline and Fall

Christmas doesn't exactly end these days. It did once. Christmas used to be twelve days of constant carousing that culminated on Twelfth Night with a big feast and maybe a play (hence the name of the Shakespeare comedy).

But now Boxing Day is simply the prelude to that weird week before New Year when nobody really knows what day it is and half the people don't go to work and the other half do, but don't seem to get much done there, and you seriously start to wonder whether it's possible to make turkey curry. Christmas, as we've seen, used to be a twelve-day holiday, and it's heading back that way. We are becoming farmers again.

Christmas doesn't end, exactly, it fades out. Or at least, the dead tree in the living room starts to look rather odd, and the baubles seem childish and the Christmas songs sound kitsch. We are embarrassed out of our festivities.

The turkey is gone the way of all flesh, and the dieting begins. Joy, love and eggnog are brushed away by the humourless hand of the cruellest of all creatures: the New Year's resolution.

And now the poetry is gone. Christmas is over, or at least that portion of Christmas with which this book is concerned. And by Twelfth Night the decorations must be packed away, the halls undecked and the Christmas tree laid outside on the street. Christmas must be put away, which is appropriate because, oddly enough, Christmas means Go Away, Christ.

People are always going on about the true meaning of Christmas and how it's been lost or forgotten or mislaid. But the etymological meaning of Christmas is Go Away, Christ, and as the etymology of the word etymology is true-meaning, that must be the true meaning of Christmas.

To understand why, you need to know that, according to the early Christians, there were four levels of religion. Level number one were the pagans. Being a pagan was a bad thing. It meant you were steeped in lust and debauchery, but it was still a bad thing. Pagans were not allowed in church.

Level number two were the inquirers, or audientes. An audiente was somebody who had once asked a Christian what this whole Jesus thing was about, who'd expressed an interest. And, just as with religions and package holidays in our own day, he would never again get a moment's peace. You see, he wasn't a pagan any more, but he wasn't a proper Christian yet either. He was on God's eternal mailing list. He was also allowed into church, but not for the services.

After a while, an audiente would get so tired of this he'd either change his name, start a persecution, or give in and ask to receive instruction. At that moment he became a catechumen. He was now allowed to come to church services, but only for the first half. He got the sermon and a few prayers, but before all the really good stuff started – the eating of the body of Christ and the drinking of the sacred blood – he was ordered out. This halfway point was the Dismissal of the Catechumens.

After two years of instruction and living without immorality or vice or any fun at all, the catechumen could be baptized. At that point he was allowed to take communion and stay the whole way through till the Dismissal of the Faithful, right at the end.

One of the really odd things about this, is

that loads of people voluntarily stayed catechumens for years longer than they needed to. St Ambrose, St Basil, St John Chrysostom and lots of others put off baptism into their thirties, and to this day nobody is quite sure why. Constantine the Great, whom everybody knows as the first Christian emperor, was only baptized on his death bed, and was therefore, technically, only a Christian emperor for a few minutes before disappearing off into death's darkness.

But I digress. The important thing here is that the Latin for the 'sending away of the catechumens' was *missa catechumenorum*. (By the way, that's the same Latin word that gave us 'mission', something you're sent away on.) So *missa catechumenorum* became the name for the whole second half of the service. Then it got shortened to *missa*. And then, slowly, it became the default word for the whole service. *Missa* in Latin, *messe* in French and in English: Mass.

In fact, the Old English sometimes called the Mass the send-ness. And they called

Christ the Haeland, or healer. So the festival could have ended up being called the Healer-Sending, which would have been rather pretty. But instead we went with the Greek Christ, meaning 'the anointed one', and the Latin *missa*, meaning 'Get out of here'.

And now it is, I suppose, time to go. We can all return to the normal course of things. That wonderful eleven-month season when we don't love our fellow human, or think of the children, or any of that silly Christmas stuff.

Epilogue

Happy, happy Christmas, that can win us back to the delusions of our childhood.

Charles Dickens, *The Pickwick Papers*

You may be wondering, dear reader, why I have said absolutely nothing at all about Christmas in foreign climes. And it's true that there are some strange and beautiful variants. In Iceland, for example, they have thirteen Father Christmases who have wonderful Icelandic names like The Window Peeper and The Sausage Thief. Indeed, the Icelandic system is arguably much better than ours from a child-control point of view. Because they deliver presents on all thirteen nights up to Christmas, a parent can actually follow through on the no-present-if-you're-naughty threat without being an utter sadist. To be precise, a child who has been naughty that day receives a rotten potato instead of a gift, which can then just be delivered the next day. The result is a fortnight of domestic peace and bliss.

Or you may have wished for an explanation of the Catalan Caga Tio, an odd log-like creature with a face that poos out presents on Christmas Eve, but only if he is savagely beaten. I too would like an explanation of the Caga Tio.

There are two reasons that I have been so insular. First, it would have made this book insufferably long, and I follow the rule of Callimachus that a big book is a big evil. Second, I probably don't have the knowledge. Of course, one can look it up. I did. I spent a happy day in the British Library reading a book from the 1960s called *Christmas the World Over* and taking notes. I learnt, for example, that in Poland presents are brought by the Star Man, but only to children who can recite their catechism.

Then, that evening, I happened to meet a real live Polish person. This was unfortunate. I like books. I understand books. But actual people terrify me. Especially female ones. Anyway, eventually I plucked up the courage and asked her who had brought the Christmas gifts to her as a child. She gave me what I can best describe as an odd look, and told me Santa.

'Not the Star Man?' I asked.

'What is the Star Man?'

'The Star Man. He brings presents to children who can recite their catechism.'

'Is this an English thing?'

'No. In Poland. I read it in a book.'

She burst out laughing. Then all her friends burst out laughing. She had never heard of the Star Man, because the Western Christmas has invaded Poland, as it is invading much of the world. All the Hollywood films and the songs and the picture books and the action figures have been slowly but inexorably forcing out national variants. This process is called globalization, according to a book I read.

And we are probably losing something. Christmas is like that. A hundred traditions have gone, and new ones have taken their place. The truth is that, for all of us, the perfect Christmas is the one of our childhood that will not come again. An annual feast will always have something missing: the empty chair at the Christmas table where somebody used to sit, who is now missing. And one day, I suppose, I shall be missing too; and you, dear reader, will be missing; and everyone we sit down with this year, old and young, will one day be missing. And the feast will continue.

That is how it always has been and must be. Things disappear, like pieces being slowly removed from a jigsaw. For children, Christmas is everything they might be given; for an adult, Christmas is everything we have lost. This is a truth that was as clear to Charles Dickens as it was to George Michael.

But even when we have exchanged our annual truths for eternal ones, Christmas will continue, because we need it, because underneath all that wrapping paper we are *doing* something important, however we choose to do it. Most things in life can be *said*. If you ask me any simple question – 'What's the capital of France?' 'When does the last train leave?' 'Would you like a drink?' – I can answer Paris, midnight and whisky. But that is all dross. There is Something Else, something much more important, and I cannot tell you what that Something Else is; and if I could tell you, it would not be worth the telling. We cannot say it, but we can, somehow, *do* it. And we do it at Christmas.

Glossary

England – Means England and Wales (my apologies to the Welsh). It does not mean Scotland. The Scottish have always been very dour about Christmas (and everything else). And Christmas Day didn't even become a public holiday in Scotland until 1958. Mind you, there is an old Orkney dialect word *bummock* that means a Christmas drink. So it can't have all been doom and gloom.

Puritans – Dylan Thomas once said that an alcoholic is someone you don't like who drinks as much as you do. The same sort of principle applies to the question of when a Protestant becomes a Puritan. There have been periods and places where what we would see as extreme Puritanism was just standard Protestantism. The definition changes over time, and I've just used Puritan to mean 'particularly Protestant for that day and age'.

Saints' days – According to the church calendar, and for that matter the Roman and Jewish calendars, a day lasts from sunset till sunset. So, for example, St Nicholas' Day (6 December) starts at sunset on 5 December and lasts until sunset on 6 December.

Turkey/Turkish – The Turks didn't arrive in what's now Turkey until the eleventh century. St Nicholas lived in Lycia and was therefore Lycian.

Xmas – Is in fact a very old spelling. In Greek Christ is spelt *Χριστός*, and can just be abbreviated to X. In Medieval English you could write about Xtians and Xtianity. I never actually mention *Xmas* in this book, but I believe that all glossaries, however short, ought to have a word beginning with X.

Bibliography

General

Connelly, Mark, *Christmas: A History*, Taurus, 2012

Foley, Daniel, *Christmas the World Over*, Chilton Book Co., 1963

Golby, J. M., and A. W. Purdue, *The Making of the Modern Christmas*, Batsford, 1986

Hopley, Claire, *The History of Christmas Food and Feasts*, Remember When, 2009

Lancaster, Bill, *The Department Store: A Social History*, Leicester University Press, 1995

Nast, Thomas, *Thomas Nast's Christmas Drawings for the Human Race*, Dover Fine Art, 2012

Nissenbaum, Stephen, *The Battle for Christmas*, Alfred A. Knopf, 1996

Restad, Penne L., *Christmas in America*, Oxford University Press, 1995

Roll, Susan K., *Towards the Origins of Christmas*, Kok Pharos, *c.*1995

Snyder, Philip V., *The Christmas Tree Book*, Viking Press, 1976

Tille, Alexander, *Yule and Christmas: Their Place in the Germanic Year*, David Nutt, 1899

Weiser, Francis X., *The Christmas Book*, Staples Press, 1954

Preface

Colbatch, Sir John, *A Dissertation concerning Mistletoe: a most wonderful specifick remedy for the cure of convulsive distempers, etc.*, William Churchill, 1719.

— *A Dissertation concerning Mistletoe: a most wonderful specifick remedy for the cure of convulsive distempers, etc. The second edition. To which is added, a second part, containing farther remarks and observations*, sold by James Roberts, 1720 [This is actually an entirely different book to the previous one]

Irving, Washington, *Old Christmas*, 1819 [I have used the title *Old Christmas* rather than the *Sketch Book* simply to make clearer a muddied publication history]

The Lady's Magazine or Entertaining Companion for the Fair Sex, Appropriated Solely for their Use and Amusement, vol. 15, Robinson, 1784

Liberman, Anatoly, 'Some Controversial Aspects of the Myth of Baldr', in *Alvissmal*, vol. 11, 2004, pp. 17–54

The Poetic Edda, Henry Adams Bellows (trans.), Princeton University Press, 1936

For Takanakuy see YouTube. Seriously.

Chapter 1: Why 25 December?

Cullmann, Oscar, *The Early Church* (ed. A. J. B. Higgins; trans. A. J. B. Higgins and S. Godman), SCMP, 1956

Ehrman, Bart D., and Zlatko Plese, *The Apocryphal Gospels*, Oxford University Press, 2011

Gunstone, John, *Christmas and Epiphany*, The Faith Press, 1967

Jenkins, Philip, *The Many Faces of Christ: The Thousand-Year Story of the Survival and Influence of the Lost Gospels*, Basic Books, 2015

The Pseudo-Cyprianic De Pascha Computus [AD 243], George Ogg (trans.), SPCK, 1955

Roberts, Revd Alexander, and James Donaldson (eds.), *The Ante-Nicene Fathers: Translations of the Writings of the Fathers Down to A. D. 325*, 1897: see especially Clement of Alexandria, *Stromata*; *The Proto-Gospel of James*; and Arnobius, *Adversus Nationes*

Vermes, Geza, *The Nativity: History and Legend*, Penguin, 2006

For Pharaoh's birthday see Genesis 40

Chapter 2: The Christmas Tree

Brunner, Brend, *Inventing the Christmas Tree* (trans. Benjamin A. Smith), Yale University Press, 2012

Jacquet, Hélène (ed.), *Christmas Plays From Oberufer* (trans. A. C. Harwood), Sophia Books, 2007

*Medieval French Plays (*trans. Richard Axton and John Stevens), Basil Blackwell, 1971

Murdoch, Brian, *Adam's Grace: Fall and Redemption in Medieval Literature*, D. S. Brewer, 2000

— *The Medieval Popular Bible: Expressions of Genesis in the Middle Ages*, D. S. Brewer, 2003

Murphy, Ronald G., *Tree of Salvation: Yggdrasil and the Cross in the North*, Oxford University Press, 2013

Perry, Joe, *Christmas in Germany*, University of North Carolina Press, 2010

Russ, Jennifer M., *German Festivals and Customs*, Wollf, 1982

'Snake in Christmas Tree Bites Mother', *The Times*, 26 December 2000

Snyder, Philip V., *The Christmas Tree Book*, Viking Press, 1976

Tille, Alexander, *Yule and Christmas: Their Place in the Germanic Year*, David Nutt, 1899

Chapter 3: Advent

Catholic University of America, *The New Catholic Encyclopedia*, 2nd edn, Gale, 2003

Crump, William D., *The Christmas Encyclopedia*, McFarland, 2001

Higgs, Michelle, *Christmas Cards: From the 1840s to the 1940s*, Shire Publishing, 1999

Russ, Jennifer M., *German Festivals and Customs*, Wolff, 1982

Chapter 4: Christmas Carols

Bolt, Rodney, *As Good as God, as Clever as the Devil: The Impossible Life of Mary Benson*, Atlantic Books, 2011

Butler, Revd Alban, *Lives of the Saints*, James Duffy, 1866

Gant, Andrew, *Christmas Carols*, Profile Books, 2014

Lawson-Jones, Revd Mark, *Why Was the Partridge in the Pear Tree?*, The History Press, 2011

Wolverton, Lisa, *Hastening Towards Prague: Power and Society in the Medieval Czech Lands*, University of Philadelphia Press, 2001

For the dating of the New Testament writing, the sources are too numerous to mention and I have merely reproduced the consensus opinions.

Chapter 5: Santa Claus: The Biography

Blount, Thomas, *Fragmenta Antiquitatis, or, Ancient Tenures of Land and Jocular Customs of Manors*, London, 1815

The Great Collection of the Lives of the Saints, vol. 2: *October* (comp. St Demetrius of Rostov; trans. Thomas Marretta), Chrysostom Press, 1995

Irving, Washington, *A History of New-York*, various editions.

Jones, Charles W., 'Knickerbocker Santa Claus', in *New-York Historical Society Quarterly*, October 1954

— *St Nicholas of Myra, Bari and Manhattan: Biography of a Legend*, University of Chicago Press, 1978

Life, Works, and Miracles of Our Holy Father Nicholas, Archbishop of Myra in Lycia (trans. John Quinn & Bryson Sewell), first half of ninth century, Bibliotheca Hagiographica Graeca 1348. (Sections 1–11 are published by and copyright the St Nicholas Center under the Creative Commons Attribution – NonCommercial-NoDerivatives 4.0. Sections 12–52 were commissioned by Roger Pearse, Ipswich, and are released by him into the public domain.)

May, Robert L., *Rudolph the Red-Nosed Reindeer*, Maxton, 1950

Webster, George P., and Thomas Nast, *Santa Claus and His Works*, McLoughlin Brothers, 1869

An excellent selection of documents on St Nicholas has been compiled online by stnicholascenter.org

Chapter 6: Christmas Dinner

MacKenzie, Neil, *The Medieval Boy Bishops*, Matador, 2012

Chapter 7: Boxing Day

Hall, Joseph, *The contemplations upon the history of the New Testament, now complete. Together with divers treatises*, 1634

The London Chronicle for 1757, vol II. June 2 to December 31, London

Roberts, Elizabeth, *A Woman's Place: An Oral History of Working Class Women 1890–1940*, Wilcy Blackwell, 1995

Epilogue

Wittgenstein, Ludwig, *Remarks on Frazer's 'Golden Bough'*, Brynmill Press, 1979

Acknowledgements

The author would like to thank Jane Seeber for her sharp eye and fine judgement; Professor Graeme Dunphy for help with the Paradise Plays; Brian Jay Jones for kindly talking me through the different editions of Irving's *A History of New-York*; Anthea Goldsmith for giving me *Old Christmas*; Michael Swift for setting me straight on Edward White Benson; and Paul Conrad, Martin Graebe and Angela Williams for help in the ultimately fruitless search for the origins of That Story, which would have made this book so much better.

Index